P9-DHT-311

*What Parents, Professionals, and Educators
are saying about the
Thinking Organized Program...*

"The book entitled *Thinking Organized* provides many wonderful ideas, practical approaches and blueprints to improve the executive functioning skills of disorganized thinkers and to help ensure their academic success. I recommend this book as important reading for parents as well as educators and pediatricians."

*Irwin L. Schwartz, M.D., F.A.A.P.,
Clinical Associate Professor of Pediatrics,
State University of New York at Stony Brook*

"It's easy for parents to get frustrated and say to the child, 'You just need to work harder and study more.' The challenge is to identify and address each child's individual needs and come up with a plan. It was never a question of working harder, it was finding a way to work smarter and more efficiently. *Thinking Organized* helped our child find the necessary strategies and skills to be a successful, lifelong learner."

Robyn Wagman, parent, Bethesda, Maryland

"*Thinking Organized for Parents and Children* is a really valuable contribution to the bookshelf of all parents who need to understand and support disorganized children. I found myself recommending it to parents immediately after reading the book in manuscript form!"

*Martha Bridge Denckla, M.D., Batza Family Endowed Chair,
Director, Developmental Cognitive Neurology,
Kennedy Krieger Institute; and Professor, Neurology, Pediatrics,
Psychiatry, Johns Hopkins University School of Medicine*

LEWIS & CLARK LIBRARY
120 S. LAST CHANCE GULCH
HELENA, MONTANA 59601

"*Thinking Organized* is an easy-to-follow guide for parents who want to help their children do better in school. I'll be sure to recommend this to the parents of my students."

Catherine Arnold, teacher, Midlothian, Virginia

"What a great resource! *Thinking Organized* is a structured approach that will work well for frustrated parents and their children."

Dr. Robert G. Gibby, Jr., PhD, Psychologist, Richmond, Virginia

"After years of helping young people overcome their problems with organization, Rhona Gordon has shared her approach in a user-friendly book. *Thinking Organized* describes strategies for time management, assignment tracking, keeping notebooks, studying, memorizing, note-taking and writing. Only someone who has worked long in the trenches could have anticipated all the usual "breakdown points" with such practical and effective suggestions. *Thinking Organized* is Rhona Gordon's gift to parents struggling to help their children learn how to learn. I will recommend it to all my patients with organizational difficulties."

Daniel Shapiro, M.D., Developmental and Behavioral Pediatrics, Rockville, Maryland

"*Thinking Organized* has helped my family live by a schedule that even my youngest children can manage."

Samantha Macholl, parent, West Palm Beach, Florida

Thinking Organized

For Parents and Children

Helping Kids Get ORGANIZED for Home, School & Play

Rhona M. Gordon, M.S., CCC/SLP

Silver Spring, MD

LEWIS & CLARK LIBRARY
120 S. LAST CHANCE GULCH
HELENA, MONTANA 59601

Thinking Organized for Parents and Children: Helping Kids Get Organized for Home, School, & Play by Rhona M. Gordon, M.S., CCC/SLP

Published by Thinking Organized,
8639-B Sixteenth Street, Ste. 290, Silver Spring, MD 20910.
Visit www.ThinkingOrganized.com for more information.

© 2007, Rhona M Gordon, Thinking Organized. All Rights Reserved.
No part of this publication may be reproduced or distributed in any form or by any means, or stored in a database or retrieval system, without the prior written permission of the publisher.

The information published in this book and any other derivative material is the opinion of the publishers only and is not meant to supplant or replace professional medical or mental healthcare, advice, or treatment in any way. Persons should always seek the advice of a professionally licensed health-care worker and consider more than one professional opinion when making decisions and choices about personal development, mental, and physical healthcare or treatment. The publishers are not responsible for any situation or outcome as a result of the personal use of the information published in this book or any other derivative material.

Cover and interior design by Pneuma Books, LLC. www.pneumabooks.com
Cover photographs courtesy of Corbis Images

Publisher's Cataloging-In-Publication Data
(Prepared by The Donohue Group, Inc.)

Gordon, Rhona M.
    Thinking organized for parents and children : helping kids get organized for home, school & play / Rhona M. Gordon.
        p. ; cm.
    Includes bibliographical references and index.

    ISBN-13: 978-0-9790034-1-7
    ISBN-10: 0-9790034-1-5

1. Students—Time management—Handbooks, manuals, etc. 2. Students—Life skills guides. 3. Study skills—Handbooks, manuals, etc. I. Title.

LB3607.8 .G67 2007
371.8   2007900789

Printed in the United States of America
12 11 10 09 08 07   6 5 4 3 2 1

This book is dedicated to the memory of my father,
Dr. Milton Gordon,
my teacher, my guide, my mentor.

Contents

Preface

From Chaos
to Success

*B*obby's parents were at their wits' end. At first they thought he was just being forgetful. Bobby could not keep up with his things. He came home without his coat (even in thirty-degree weather), left his schoolbooks in his locker, and often could not find his assignment notebook. He was considered a bright boy and could talk with enthusiasm and authority about the many characters in his video game. However, when it was time to start his homework, Bobby seemed to fall apart. He procrastinated and did not know where to begin. This caused him to become frustrated and overwhelmed even with routine assignments. The last straw was when Bobby and his parents worked for hours on a science paper, really struggling to follow the directions and spell every word correctly. Much to everyone's surprise, Bobby "forgot" to hand in the paper, resulting in a grade of zero. When questioned by his parents and teacher, he claimed he could not find the paper in his backpack.

Bobby's parents watched his frustration build as he struggled to manage his daily tasks. Bobby began to complain that school was "too hard" and that he was "stupid." After a series of tutors and some failing grades, Bobby's parents enlisted our help to teach him better organizational and study skills.

Initially, Bobby was quite resistant to trying new strategies to manage his work. He felt there was no real reason for him to change because he had a system in place. Even though his existing system was not really helping him, Bobby did not want to try something new. This is frequently one of the challenges of helping disorganized students. I knew I could not give up on Bobby nor could I allow him to maintain his old system. It was not working. He was struggling, his grades were poor, and he was losing confidence in his abilities.

During our time together, I required Bobby to follow the Thinking Organized program. At home his parents reinforced the strategies we practiced in therapy. Bobby was rewarded for compliance with the program and started having fun e-mailing me after finishing a task. Soon, Bobby began to see an improvement in his grades.

One week, Bobby came to me worried about an upcoming history exam. He felt there was just too much information to remember. Furthermore, the history textbook was difficult to read and quite boring. But Bobby really wanted to do well on this test. We started studying a week ahead of time by creating outlines that separated main ideas from supporting details and drawing timelines for historical events. Bobby had fun creating a silly song to memorize facts. We broke his studying into parts and scheduled each task. Bobby reviewed the material independently and was able to follow the established schedule with little assistance. He agreed to a final review with his father in which they worked on predicting essay questions and preparing hypothetical outlines. By the day of the test, Bobby felt confident that he had done a good job preparing.

I always tell my students that feeling ready for a test is more important than the actual grade. I know most of them do not believe me. However, I have found that with continued use of proper studying strategies, grades begin to reflect these good efforts.

Seeing confidence in a student like Bobby makes me determined to share these strategies with other students. For the past thirty years, I have seen firsthand how difficult school can be for some students. Some have formal diagnoses, others have been labeled as just plain lazy, and still others say they "just don't care." *I disagree*. I have never met a student who does not want to succeed in school. Some do not know how to study, and some are unwilling to commit the time, but I have never met a student who does not want to get an A.

The Thinking Organized program was developed to make it possible for *parents* to help a disorganized student. Although I would like to personally work with each and every student, I know that there are only twenty-four hours in the day. Therefore, it was imperative that I create a tool that a parent could use to help a struggling child.

The Thinking Organized program has proven its success over the years. Even if the students do not seem to remember the strategies you have taught, most students remember them when they need them.

One of my favorite examples is Nina, who resisted using much of the Thinking Organized program in high school. I knew that Nina had learned the skills but was choosing not to use them. She called me after her freshman year in college to report that her grades were not what she had hoped. Nina promised that next year would be better. During the first semester of her sophomore year, I received a picture of Nina's dorm room. Her wall was covered with color-coded calendars and study guides. I am happy to report that Nina's grades did improve. Most importantly, she was pleased with herself for implementing the skills she had been taught to achieve her academic goals.

The road from chaotic thinking to Thinking Organized is not straight or easy. There are many curves and turns along the way. However, children, teenagers, and adults CAN learn the strategies to effectively organize their thinking and their world.

A NOTE ON GENDER

In my practice, I work with many children, both boys and girls. I wanted to represent all students in this book and therefore have chosen to alternate the use of masculine and feminine pronouns by chapter.

Ackowledgments

Thank You!

This book is a labor of love born out of thirty years of helping children, young adults, and parents. The first people I must thank are all of the students who have worked so hard on the very things that are toughest for them and in the process, helped me to refine a set of strategies that can be used for the benefit of others. Special thanks are also extended to the parents of our students for believing in the Thinking Organized program and never giving up on their children.

Thinking Organized could not have helped so many students without the extremely high caliber of dedication and service exhibited by my wonderful staff of speech pathologists, educational mentors, and administrative personnel. Their clinical contributions and confidence in the strategies have made our program successful.

I thank the professionals and parents who have taken their time to read the manuscript and am greatly appreciative of their valuable insights. A special thanks to Ann Litt, author of *Eating Well on Campus*, for her advice and support.

A huge debt of gratitude is owed to my brilliant editor, Sherry Sall. Her ability to translate clinical information into readable text has enabled me to complete this project while maintaining my practice.

My children and granddaughter — Shira, Jessica, Jeremy, and Michelle — have been a source of strength and inspiration throughout the writing process. I am also thankful for the unending love and support of my entire family: sisters, brother-in-laws, nieces, and nephews. Thank you to my dear mother, who has always believed in me and any project I undertake. Her uncanny instincts and calming personality have been a guiding force in my life. Finally, I would like to thank my father, the most wonderful and caring pediatrician that I have ever met. He taught me patience and perseverance and instilled in me the firm belief that even the most challenging child can be successful.

Getting Started

Thinking Organized

*E*very parent knows how difficult and stressful it can be getting the kids off to school each morning. Time is tight and any small problem can upset the schedule. A misplaced textbook or sweater can lead to missing the bus. Not only does being disorganized affect the child who missed the bus, it impacts the morning routine for the rest of the family. Mom may be late for work and other siblings may be late for school. This can lead to a tearful, stressful beginning of the day.

What will it take to get a smoother morning routine? A better memory? More time? Greater organization? The answer is found in a term you may never have heard of:

executive functions. Improving executive functions can be the solution to a bad start to the day.

Within the same family, you may have one child who is quite organized, while another is forgetful, frequently late, and always missing belongings. The difference may be the level of the child's executive functioning skills. Either the child organizes herself, or a parent has to be the constant watchdog. If you're currently acting like the watchdog, I'm here to help. Any child's executive functions can be improved, and the techniques in this book will help you achieve that goal. First let's take a closer look at exactly what executive functioning skills really do.

TOOLS FOR LIFE

Executive functions are a set of skills needed by each individual to set goals, organize a plan to meet those goals, and effectively complete activities within a given time frame. A person uses executive functions to create modifications to the plan when circumstances require change. Executive functions stem from the frontal lobes of the brain and work as the manager of everyday life. They are the skills that an executive uses to run a busy office. A parent uses many executive functioning skills in order to manage the morning rush. Mom or Dad know what time to wake the children and how long each one needs to shower and dress; Mom and Dad also help organize backpacks and get the children to school on time.

Children are also required to be mindful of time, keep track of their belongings, and utilize a variety of executive functioning skills to meet their daily obligations. Consider a fifth grade student who wants to invite a friend to her house.

If she calls the friend ten minutes before she wants to play, chances are the friend will not be available. However, if the child calls the night before, there is a greater likelihood that they can get together. In school, students learn executive functioning skills when they are very young. Even in pre-kindergarten, children learn how to prioritize, where to store materials, and how to follow a daily schedule. As children get older, they are required to organize, monitor, and manage their time and materials independent of their parents and teachers.

Executive functioning skills form the underlying basis for successful academic achievement. From simple tasks such as managing supplies to more complex ones such as writing a research paper, the ability to plan, monitor, revise, and complete an activity is crucial. Adults working in a job are required to learn and repeat skills that are similar from day to day. Children must remember many different facts from a variety of disciplines, even those that hold no interest for them personally. Not only are students required to learn and memorize large chunks of material, they are expected to form ideas and concepts from that material and present it in an organized format — a tall order for a disorganized thinker.

Every day, parents and children come into my office because of executive functioning weaknesses, although most people do not label it this way. Many students complain that their grades were fine in elementary school, but life is so much more challenging in middle school and high school. One of the biggest transitions for a middle school student is to manage multiple subjects and requirements, let alone get to the locker and classroom on time.

After the first month of school, when Bethany was getting penalized for not handing in assignments, she started carrying all her books and papers in her backpack so she would not lose anything. Although this system guaranteed that she would have her materials, Bethany never seemed to have the right notebook out at the right time. She spent a lot of time fishing through her backpack and over the weeks her frustration grew. When she and her mother recognized that her system was not working, Bethany came to my office for help.

This example and the others in this book come from the many wonderful students and parents with whom I work. I hope the examples here help you to see that you're not alone. Other families are struggling with the same issues. Sometimes parents and teachers feel a child is just not motivated, or that she is lazy and that she really does not care. That's why this program works. If a child seems lazy, it could be because she's learned that behavior to compensate for her lack of ability to help herself stay organized.

If organization and time management come easily to you, it may be hard to believe that your child finds it to be such a struggle. But the truth is that some students really do not know how to initiate and maintain systems of organization, even if they are at an age where they "should" be using effective systems. Many students have told me that when school gets hard, sometimes it feels like it's easier to give up than to keep "hitting their head against the wall."

Frequently, students come to my office and say, "I don't really care about how I do in school." They add, "I don't really know how to do it differently." What that says to me loud and clear is that they've tried numerous systems and nothing seems to work, so it's easier to just give up.

Let's look at an example of executive functioning difficulties in a middle school student. Johnny doesn't get out of bed unless he's pulled out. His parents have tried setting two separate alarms, waking him with a favorite CD, and taking away privileges; but they have resigned themselves to dragging him out of bed. He is cranky getting dressed, doesn't like to eat breakfast, and cannot seem to locate his backpack. Frequently, the morning begins with his parents being angry with him for forgetting homework, leaving a book behind, or being dressed for seventy-degree weather when it's only forty. Furthermore, his actions make his siblings late, and they find themselves leaving the house in a screaming match. This is why parents and children long for summer vacation when schedules are more relaxed and everyone in the family seems to be kinder and friendlier.

Just last weekend, I listened to a mother discuss her frustration with trying to find a way to help her four children organize their work and get it done. Each of her children is at a different stage and the strategies that worked well for the oldest are not working for her siblings. So what's a parent to do?

As children get older, teachers in school are less willing to serve as their executive functioning partners. They require students to manage their own time and work. Teachers are usually available when a student has a question and brings it to their attention. However, the disorganized student may not realize that she has questions until the night before the test or may be reluctant to approach the teacher.

I like to look at a child who acts resistant as a child who doesn't have the tools to be her own self-advocate. When she learns to think far enough ahead to get questions answered early, confusion decreases, studying runs more smoothly, and test performance improves. This ultimately leads to a student feeling better about her abilities.

It's easy to see that life with executive functioning weaknesses becomes a vicious cycle. Parents become frustrated with their child, the child becomes frustrated with herself, and then the parents grow more frustrated because they have not found a way to help their child. Sound familiar?

THE GOOD NEWS

Children as well as adults present with similar organizational difficulties, just at different levels. The third grader is worried about handing in homework and studying. The adult must find a way to schedule appointments and maintain an effective calendar to keep up with events and activities. Although there are general disorganized traits frequently seen in individuals with executive functioning weaknesses, each person presents in slightly different ways.

Most everyone has heard the terms *Attention Deficit Disorder* (*ADD*) or *Attention Deficit Hyperactivity Disorder* (*ADHD*). These terms were not available thirty years ago but today are widely used to signify a lack of focus and attention. These disorders have been recognized by the medical community and have diagnostic codes. However, the medical community has differing opinions about whether executive functioning difficulties form a separate disorder. Many neurologists and pediatricians believe that weaknesses presented in executive functioning are related to other disorders. For example, a student who has a diagnosis of ADD or a written language disability may have executive functioning difficulties stemming from her other problems.

No matter what you call it and whether or not you have a formal diagnosis, it is clear that executive functioning weaknesses can be a significant detriment not only to the student, but to the entire family. It is an area that needs consistent attention and practice until new skills become habits.

Luckily, executive functioning skills *can* be taught; and with enough practice and reinforcement, the habits of a disorganized thinker can be changed. The Thinking Organized program has been developed over years of working with students of varying ages and abilities. In this book, six aspects of effective executive functioning skills are introduced, expanded, and practiced: material organization, time management, studying strategies, memory techniques, note-taking for reading comprehension, and written language. I understand the troubles that families are facing; therefore, the Thinking Organized program addresses those areas that are consistently more difficult for the disorganized student.

DO WE NEED PROFESSIONAL HELP?

In many ways, a parent working directly with a child is the best way to bring about dramatic changes in her executive functioning skills. One reason is that parents can reinforce the skills on a daily basis and demonstrate them by verbal modeling. For example, a parent could include the child in planning the day's schedule by saying, "Aunt Susan's wedding is this weekend and your poster is due at school on Monday. So today, I need to pick up the dry cleaning and your poster board. We are low on dog food and milk, so how should I plan my day? I have to get the milk last, because it will spoil if left in the car, and I need to be back by two to let in the handyman." The parent can then help the child apply the same skills to her academic work, breaking larger tasks into smaller ones and prioritizing assignments.

Another advantage the parent has is more informal

time with the child. Strategies to improve executive functioning skills can be built into daily life. For example, a child can practice memory strategies by helping in the grocery store. While in the produce section, ask your child to get five different items. Demonstrate how the items can be grouped into categories, such as type of food, color, or size. Quick, informal challenges such as this one demonstrate that good executive functioning skills are needed in all aspects of life. When the Thinking Organized program is integrated with both schoolwork and home activities, the skills practiced become lifetime organizational habits.

However, children (and parents) are individuals with different strengths and weaknesses. Sometimes students who have struggled in school are very motivated and will quickly recognize the benefits of learning to think organized. Other children resist interference from their parents and seem to give more credence to a third party. It is possible that further assistance will be needed to establish effective organizational strategies for your child. There are several resources available to you. Some are listed in the appendix of this book and on our website **www.thinkingorganized.com**.

The time spent teaching the Thinking Organized skills is always beneficial for the student, even if you decide you need outside help with the program. Any improvement in executive functioning skills that a parent fosters in a child can become a strong motivator. Success breeds success. As her grades improve, the student becomes more confident and uses the strategies more consistently.

THE VALUE OF REPETITION

The Thinking Organized program aims to provide the ideal

environment for improving executive functioning skills. The reality of working with disorganized and sometimes resistant students frequently tempers the goals of each strategy. Do not despair! Repetition is necessary for students to internalize skills, and if a goal is not met immediately, keep at it. Emphasize that the systems must be used and that they will help the student save time, improve her grades, and start Thinking Organized!

Mrs. M. came to me extremely frustrated because she'd been trying to help her son get organized each night before bed. Together they put all the material into the backpack and closed it for the evening. The next day Mom put the lunch in the backpack and closed it quickly. But every morning as they drove to school, there was a backpack explosion! Only half of the papers that left the house in the morning were in the child's bag once he got to school. This mother was at her wit's end. She felt that she had done everything possible to be sure her child got to school with all his belongings.

My first job was convincing Mrs. M. that her child was not doing this on purpose. Next, we devised a simple system. We decided the mom would close the child's backpack with a twist tie after putting in his lunchbox. This eliminated the temptation for the child to see what was in his backpack on the way to school. Therefore, once he got to school he still had everything he needed. Both mom and child were much happier and less frustrated.

HOW TO MOTIVATE YOUR CHILD

It is difficult to change any habit. Initially, the Thinking Organized program can take some effort. Most students soon realize the benefits of organizing their thoughts and materials and are intrinsically motivated to improve their grades. However, to effectively replace deeply ingrained habits, a system of rewards greatly facilitates daily implementation of the new Thinking Organized routine.

All adults who deal with children develop strategies to shape behavior. A mother praises her toddler's first steps and a teacher may reward mastery of multiplication facts with an ice cream party. Psychological research has proven that behavior that is rewarded or reinforced tends to be repeated. Unacknowledged behavior tends to diminish or disappear. The principles of behavior modification are simply a formal method that observes behavior and seeks to shape it in positive ways.

Communication is an important part of the process. The student needs to know exactly what is expected of her. Each goal should be realistic and achievable. When she encounters failure, show her how to correct the mistake and move on. Be quick to praise her for her efforts. Verbal praise and recognition are important reinforcements that encourage the child to keep trying.

The Thinking Organized program clearly outlines the goals for each strategy. Create an individualized reward program for your child, or use one of the suggestions below:

- *Charts* can be a visual reminder of the student's progress. Colorful charts help focus on accomplishments instead of punishing poor performance. A star or a checkmark for each day the student correctly writes down assignments could add up to a reward or privilege at the end of the week.
- *Activity rewards* can represent extra privileges, such as picking a favorite board game, going to the playground, or playing games on the computer.

- ***Tangible rewards***, such as small toys or treats, should be used in moderation to remain effective. One idea is to give the child collectible rewards such as baseball or trading cards, doll clothes, or coins from other countries. Alternatively, the reward can have several parts to be given over time: for example, parts of a model airplane or Lego® kit. An older student is more likely to be motivated by something she can choose herself, such as a gift certificate for a video rental, fast food, or clothing store. The student can earn points for mastering each strategy to be applied toward the gift certificate.
- ***Token rewards*** are beneficial because they immediately reinforce positive behavior without interrupting the flow of the lesson. Tokens can be exchanged for a reward when the child masters each strategy.

Each child should only be competing with herself. Therefore, if more than one child is involved in the Thinking Organized program, be sure that each individual chart or record of progress is kept private so that each student marks her own achievements, rather than competing with a sibling. When struggling students are working on improving their organizational skills, competition between peers or siblings is not an effective motivator. However, praise for small increments of progress reinforces the student's positive feelings about her achievement and encourages continued efforts to stick to the program.

Some people call this goal setting. In the initial process, the parent will guide the goal setting by determining the tasks and deadline for completion. As the child becomes better at managing her day, the parent should gradually allow her to set the goals. At this stage, the parent should oversee the child's progress, refocusing her if additional help is needed. For example, Cheryl's tenth grader announced that he was tired of his mother "nagging" him and wanted to manage his schoolwork himself. She made a contract with her son that as long as his grades were Bs and Cs, he could maintain his work independently. When she noticed online that his grades were below Cs, she was allowed to step in and monitor his assignments and binder more closely. The ultimate goal is for the student to record and complete work independently; however, some students require gradual steps to reach this goal.

Another important tool to foster is self-advocacy, which is the student's ability to identify when she is struggling to understand something and to seek out the help of a teacher to clarify that information. It can be extremely difficult for a student to approach a teacher to ask for help. Often the disorganized student does not think about the teacher as a good resource, or she waits until the night before a test to study, too late to ask for help. It can be a scary proposition for a student to risk asking a "stupid" question. However, it is important to encourage the student to get help as soon as information becomes confusing. The reason can be explained in my standard "house foundation" lecture. If you are building a house and have holes in the foundation, the floors above it will be shaky. If you fill those holes as soon as you spot them, your house will be secure. The same holds true for the learner. She will be better able to grasp information if she has used resources to help clarify confusing material.

Once a child becomes comfortable with the Thinking Organized program, the system of reinforcements may naturally discontinue. Many students grow more self-motivated

Toward Independence!

*A*lthough this book helps you teach your child necessary skills to negotiate daily life, the ultimate goal is for the child to manage life independently. In order to do that, most of these skills need to be routinized and become an integral part of how your student handles each task. Once the skills become habit, most students are encouraged by their success and continue using the strategies independently. However, in the beginning, effective reinforcers are necessary to help your student feel good about her proper use of the Thinking Organized program.

as their grades improve and they recognize the effectiveness of the strategies. However, there may still be a discrepancy between parental expectations and the student's level of independence. It is clear that the earlier effective organizational strategies are introduced and reinforced with a child, the more likely she will be to integrate them effectively when she wants to succeed.

HOW TO BEGIN?

There are six strategies in the Thinking Organized program. Some parents tackle one chapter each week; others find their children need more time to practice. Therefore, you really must establish your own schedule based on how well your child understands each strategy. Regardless of your schedule, it is not necessary to read the whole book before you begin. It is perfectly acceptable to read each chapter just before working with your child.

Children with organizational difficulties are not all the same. One student may have considerable trouble with time management but no problem maintaining her materials. For this child, the parent may want to quickly review the chapter on material organization but spend more time practicing the strategies of time management. If you feel that your child is strong in an area, review that chapter briefly. Plan to spend most of your time practicing the strategies that address your child's specific areas of weakness.

THINKING ORGANIZED RESOURCES

Handouts and worksheets are available for each of the six strategies of the Thinking Organized program. These tools will help you establish and implement the Thinking Organized program in your own home easily and successfully.

To order, visit **www.thinkingorganized.com**.

Strategy 1

Material Organization

*M*aterial organization is a system of storing your belongings in an orderly fashion so that they are accessible when needed. This is an extremely important component of an organized life and a necessary skill for academic success. An efficient student properly documents and monitors assignments and establishes a system of maintaining books, papers, and supplies.

When John was a high school freshman, he did not see the need to file his papers. Although his mother offered to give him file folders and help him establish a system, John insisted on keeping all his papers for school stuffed into one binder. He believed that his system was adequate because he saved all of the papers and knew where they were. As the year progressed, John's binder became increasingly full and disorganized. His mother became frustrated as she saw papers hanging out the side of the binder and getting ripped. When it was time to study for his final exams, John began to organize his papers and quickly realized that he was in trouble. He was missing an important timeline for his history exam. A math quiz he wanted to review had gotten wet and was unreadable. John reported that it took him more than eight hours over two days to sort through his jumbled mess, find additional papers that were loose in his desk, and establish what material was missing. The weekend before exams, he lost so much time organizing that he did not have time to study properly.

The next year, John followed the Thinking Organized filing system from day one. When it was time for finals, he opened his drawer and quickly found the papers he needed filed neatly in subject folders. John called to report how wonderful he felt to not have "that panicky feeling" before exams. He was able to jump right into studying with confidence that he was not missing any important material.

Material organization is the first strategy introduced in the Thinking Organized program because students need an effective system to keep track of assignments and paperwork. This is a baseline skill in the organizational process. It is very difficult to do well in school if a student is missing homework sheets, assignments, or study guides or if he lacks a clear system for documenting and monitoring his assignments.

It is important for the student to use the structures introduced in this chapter every day in order for the skills to become routinized. Even if the student does not like the system, it is important to insist on daily adherence in order to establish effective material organization. First we'll look at the goals for each strategy and how to prepare. Then we'll discuss how to get the student involved. Let's get to work.

GOALS

Material organization is a key component of executive functioning and a necessity for success in school. When a student learns to document assignments and has a system for keeping track of his materials, he saves time and lessens frustration. The goals for this strategy are to establish three systems:

1. *Assignment notebook:* The parent will help the student set up an assignment notebook and learn how to use it to document his work. Proper use of the assignment notebook is difficult, so plan to check the notebook after school each day and devote time to improving entries.

2. *Binder:* A system for keeping the student's papers neatly organized will help save time when preparing to complete an assignment or study for a test.

3. *Other materials:* To help the student keep up with his personal belongings, a dedicated area will be established for items needed every day, such as keys, cell phone, and backpack.

PREPARATION

Before beginning to teach your child the components of proper material organization, you will need to organize your supplies.

1. *Assignment notebook*: Frequently, schools have their

own assignment notebooks that the students must use. If not, then choose a notebook with wide spaces for entries and margins for notes.

2. *Pens*: Purchase red, blue, black, and green pens to help the child color-code his notebook.

3. *Binder*: Purchase one of the following systems to maintain the student's papers.

   • Some teachers require that the student use a three-ring binder. If so, provide one two-pocket folder for each subject to help with papers that are not hole-punched.

   • Older students sometimes prefer to use an accordion folder. If so, purchase a six- or twelve-pocket folder and labels.

   • If the student chooses to have a separate notebook for each subject, be sure to choose notebooks with pocket folders to help keep his papers neat.

4. *An area for other materials*: Establish an area for your child to put everyday things, such as his keys, cell phone, and backpack. This will become the first place he stops when arriving home and the last place he'll check before leaving the house again.

GOAL 1: ASSIGNMENT NOTEBOOK

Keeping a properly ordered assignment notebook is critical to effective organization and time management. First, introduce the rules to the student and explain how to set up and maintain the notebook. Alert your child that this is something you will be checking each day after school and that it is a necessary skill for academic success. If possible, ask the teachers to check the notebook in each class and initial it after each period. Consistent use of an assignment notebook is a *crucial* step, and once the student internalizes this, notebook use will become an integral part of his organization and he will not want to be without it.

No Choice, No Excuse

Each student MUST have an assignment notebook. As we've discussed, it's a central component of material organization. Your student may be unaccustomed to using an assignment notebook and may offer a variety of excuses to get out of keeping one. A "good memory" is not an acceptable substitute for learning the skill of writing homework in a central place. Your student may ask to use a palm pilot; however, experience has proven that palm pilots are fun for a short time, but they do not get used effectively. Internet postings of school assignments are another possible excuse your student may offer. Those can help students anticipate what's coming up in the next week, but they're no substitute for an assignment notebook. In fact, online postings from teachers can be inconsistent, outdated, or incomplete.

The student should not be given a choice about using the assignment notebook. Often, the student resists using the assignment notebook in the beginning of the course. However, keep insisting that assignment notebook rules be followed. Emphasize to your child that consistently recording assignments will ultimately save him time and increase productivity. Parents can model this strategy by sharing a personal "To Do" list.

Plan One Month Ahead

Write the subjects and the dates in the assignment notebook for an entire month. Some assignment notebooks have the

© 2007, Rhona M. Gordon, Thinking Organized. All Rights Reserved. Duplication Prohibited.

🧠	Monday 12/3	Tuesday 12/4	Wednesday 12/5	Thursday 12/6	Friday 12/7	Saturday 12/8	Sunday 12/9
Math							
English							
Science							
Spanish							
Geography							

Table 1.1 **Assignment Notebook Framework**

dates and subjects listed on the top or side of the notebook. If that is the case, then the only things you might have to add are extra courses that are not listed. For example, foreign languages are usually not listed, but extra boxes are provided so that the student can write in additional classes. A student should not list subjects where homework is never or rarely given. Use the extra sections for such times when an assignment is posted. Table 1.1 illustrates what the framework of an assignment notebook should look like.

Don't Forget!

Create a "Don't Forget" section in the assignment notebook. The "Don't Forget" section should be a place of importance, so put it at the bottom or the top of the assignment notebook where there is extra room. Label the section using bold, black ink. After the student writes an assignment in a

© 2007, Rhona M. Gordon, Thinking Organized. All Rights Reserved. Duplication Prohibited.

	Monday 12/3	Tuesday 12/4	Wednesday 12/5	Thursday 12/6	Friday 12/7	Saturday 12/8	Sunday 12/9
Math							
English							
Science							
Spanish							
Geography							
Don't Forget							

Table 1.2 **Assignment Notebook Framework with "Don't Forget" Section**

subject, he then goes to the "Don't Forget" section and adds any materials needed to complete that assignment that are not already in the binder. For example, the student gets a math assignment and writes it in the "math" section of the assignment notebook. Additionally, the teacher gives handouts with practice problems. These individual pieces of paper get placed into the binder and then there is nothing else needed to complete the homework for that evening. However, if the teacher also assigns problems from the textbook, then the textbook must be listed in the "Don't Forget" section. The student continues to list homework and textbooks needed for the other subjects. At the end of the day, the student checks the "Don't Forget" section and can quickly see which textbooks or materials are needed for nightly work.

© 2007, Rhona M. Gordon, Thinking Organized. All Rights Reserved. Duplication Prohibited.

	Monday 12/3	Tuesday 12/4	Wednesday 12/5	Thursday 12/6	Friday 12/7	Saturday 12/8	Sunday 12/9
Math							
English							
Science							
Spanish							
Geography							
Don't Forget							
Extra-Curricular							

Table 1.3 **Assignment Notebook Framework with Extracurricular Commitments**

Extracurricular Commitments

Because students these days are so busy, it's important to create a section in the assignment notebook for extracurricular commitments. Include any after-school activities, such as sports, religious school, tutoring, or chores at home. This helps the student document all obligations and keep them listed in one spot. Additionally, if a student is involved in an activity that requires extra equipment, books, or musical instruments, these should be listed in this section to help the student remember to take the needed items with him.

Complete Each Box Every Day

Each box in the assignment notebook that has a subject listed must be completed each day. In other words, if the student does not have nightly homework in a particular subject and if there is no long-term project or test/quiz for which to study, the student should mark the section "None." This decreases ambiguity, giving the student confidence that he did not miss an assignment. If a student has a test to prepare for, he cannot simply write the word "study." Often, a student will write "study" in the assignment notebook for five days. This is not really helpful, because this vague term does not divide the information into manageable chunks to help him properly prepare for an exam. Help the student list specific pieces of work to study during the course of a week. For example, if there is a history exam, the student might make lists or note cards of the key terms on the first night and then do a review section from the end of the chapter on the second night.

Color Coding Is Key

All the information in the student's assignment notebook should be color coded. This plays a valuable part in the organization of the assignment notebook. Some students like to use a lot of bright colors throughout the notebook, but that can be confusing to the eye. When the number of colors is limited and clearly defined, the student can quickly identify what work needs to be completed. Color coding works as follows:

- **RED** = Test or quiz
- BLUE = Long-term project
- **BLACK** = Nightly homework
- GREEN = Fun activities

Tests, quizzes, and long-term projects must be divided and marked in the assignment notebook. (Documenting long-term projects is further discussed in Strategy 2: Time Management.)

Check and Cross-Check
Show your student how to create and use a check/cross-check box. The student will use this box when he has completed his homework. This helps him remember that not only does the homework have to be completed, but it has to be returned to the binder to take to school the following day. Here's how to do it:
- Draw a small box in the top right corner of each subject area.
- Tell the student to put a check in the box when an assignment has been finished.
- Instruct the student to cross-check the box when the assignment has been packed in his binder.

Keeping Track
Sign the student's assignment notebook every day. The disorganized student needs help learning the rules followed by an organized student, including extra repetition and encouragement. If possible, the teacher should review what the student has written in the assignment notebook and then initial it. Sometimes the teacher does not have the time to sign an assignment notebook. If this is the case, see if there is someone else in the school who could check the notebook at the end of the day. Guidance counselors, assistants, or an older student can sometimes help ensure that a student leaves school knowing that his assignment notebook is complete and accurate.

The parent should sign the assignment notebook after the child has finished all of his work. (See figure 1.1 for an example.) In an ideal setting, the assignment notebook should be signed as the parent reviews the homework that has been placed in the binder. The parent would then watch

Toward Independence!

*W*hen establishing rules for a binder and assignment notebook, a great deal of initial monitoring is necessary. The teacher might need to sign the assignment notebook daily and the parent will review it on a nightly basis. As the student becomes more proficient at documenting assignments and filing papers, a once-a-week meeting time can be scheduled to monitor his continued use. It is important to choose a time and strictly observe it each week. Some prefer to choose Thursday night in case the weekend is needed to buy supplies for the upcoming week. Others prefer Sunday morning when they can leisurely plan the week ahead. Whatever time you choose, be sure it is convenient and practical for you to observe each week without fail.

the child put the assignment notebook into the backpack. The parent should then zip the backpack and tell the child not to open it again until he is in school.

Assignment Notebook Rules

Tape these rules to the inside of the assignment notebook. This will help the student keep track of his assignment notebook responsibilities.

1. Fill in the "Don't Forget" section.

© 2007, Rhona M. Gordon, Thinking Organized. All Rights Reserved. Duplication Prohibited.

	Monday 12/3	Tuesday 12/4	Wednesday 12/5	Thursday 12/6	Friday 12/7	Saturday 12/8	Sunday 12/9
Math	P. 123 - even only. Re-read text of chapter 3 for test	P. 123 - odd only. Redo all missed ques-tions from chapter 3 homework.	Take out of chapter test	FINAL REVIEW Reread chap 3 & rework hardest problems	Chap 3 Test Homework read until chap 4	2 PM - do math reading	
English	None	Make index cards of poetry terms	Date with Mom to call out poetry terms	final review of poetry terms	Poetry Test no homework	12:30 - Go to library to get book for report	
Science	read chapter 2 pgs 15-20	Chap 2 pgs 21-30 Research 3 different types of butterflies for project	List out features of butterflies. Start drawing pictures	Finish drawings & check project for grammar / spelling	Butterfly project due Homework: read pg 4-10 in chap 5		2 PM -- science reading
Spanish	Date with Mom to shop for ingredients	make Enchiladas tonight	SPANISH FOOD PROJECT DUE	None	no homework		2:30 review vocabulary list from last week
Geography	get blank maps for practice -- make cards for capitals	practice filling in map. Make up memory trick	Have Mom practice with capital cards -- recite memory trick for Mom	Review all cards & practice filling in map	ASIA TEST no homework.		
PE	none	None	none	NONE	None		
Don't Forget	Math book. Science book	Math book. Science book	Math book. Science book. HOCKEY GEAR.	Poetry handouts. Geography Book. Math book.	Math book. Science book. Bring in TV Guide!	Get/make contacts for Youth Group	pack book. Report book. math & science
Extra-Curricular			Hockey game after school	Hockey practice	Dinner with Grandparents	Hockey game 11:00 AM	Youth group 6 PM
Teacher's Signature	Mrs. Smith	Mrs. Smith	Mrs. Smith	Mrs. Smith	Mrs. Smith		
Parent's Signature	Mr. John Doe	Mr. John Doe	Mr. John Doe	Mr. John Doe	Mr. John Doe		

Figure 1.1 **Sample Assignment Notebook with Check/Cross-check and Signatures**

2. Color code all information:
   - **Red** = Test or quiz
   - **Blue** = Long-term project
   - **Black** = Nightly homework
   - **Green** = Fun activities
3. Complete every box every day. If there is no homework, write "NONE" in the box.
4. Fill in extracurricular activities.
   - Include any tutoring, sports, clubs, or religious school.
5. Create and use a check/cross-check box.
   - Check when done with the assignment.
   - Cross-check when assignment is packed in binder.
6. Ask Mom or Dad to sign the assignment notebook every night.
   - They can only sign when steps 1-5 have been completed.

GOAL 2: BINDER

The binder can be a nightmare for anyone with organizational difficulties. Some schools or teachers insist on a specific system for the binder; however, it may be beneficial to request a modification of that system to better fit the needs of your child. In general, the traditional three-ring binder, where each subject has its own divider and papers are filed behind the divider, does *not* work for the disorganized student.

There are several alternative ways to house a student's material, and it is important to let the student try different strategies. As a student matures and does a better job of organizing independently, the system for carrying papers may also change. We'll explore the options here.

The Traditional Binder

If the student must use a three-ring binder, then provide one two-pocket folder for each subject. A folder alleviates the problem of having to frequently open the binder rings and deal with papers that are not hole-punched. The left side of each folder is reserved for current work: homework, work in progress, or handouts currently being reviewed in class. The right side of the folder is for completed work to be taken home and filed. To create a "perfect" binder, the student would hole-punch completed papers and place them behind the appropriate subject folder. One advantage of the three-ring binder is that it can also hold a supply pouch, which should be regularly stocked with sharpened pencils, erasers, pens, and highlighters.

The parent should help the student clean out each section of the binder on a regular basis. Initially it is ideal to do this task daily. For the older student, completed papers should be placed in a labeled manila folder and stored in either a file drawer or a box in the student's room. As the student begins to file papers independently, he can be rewarded with just a weekly check. If the filing system deteriorates, then the next week the student must again clean out the binder each day with the parent. Choose a specific time for this task and be consistent. If the older student resists parental supervision, require a weekly clean out before weekend fun begins.

Keep in mind that many children continue to struggle with the three-ring binder because the task of maintaining three-hole-punched papers and dividers can be burdensome.

Accordion File

Students should purchase a six- or thirteen-section accordion binder, not the larger ones used by accountants. Choose one that closes completely with a zipper or clasp. The assignment notebook is placed in the front of the file and the last section is used for extra paper. Label the sections in the order of your child's classes and file papers so the most current ones are in the front. Many students like using the first section for homework that is to be turned in the next day. Although the accordion file is effective for many students because there are no holes to punch, be aware that papers may pile up, requiring consistent daily or weekly cleaning.

Separate Notebooks for Each Subject

High school students like this system because they can take one spiral notebook to each class rather than carrying large, clumsy binders throughout the day. Make sure the notebooks have at least one pocket in front and that the sheets are perforated for easy tear-out.

GOAL 3: OTHER MATERIALS

Disorganized students have difficulty keeping track of all their possessions, including sweaters, coats, lunch boxes, and more. In order to improve general material organization, ask your child to visualize "becoming one with his things." Your child may benefit from a daily "pat-down," running through a mental checklist of glasses, wallet, cell phone, homework, and sweater. Another effective technique is to encourage your child to use hooks or Velcro snaps on his backpack to secure his lunch box or extra clothing. If the article is firmly attached to the backpack, it is much more likely to make it home.

    In your child's room, it is helpful to establish a dedicated location for items needed every day, such as keys, cell phone, and wallet. This should be near the door and your child should "check in" at this location when leaving or arriving home. A younger child may benefit from a designated spot near the front door for all his things (jacket, lunch box, etc.).

Material organization is a stumbling block for many with executive function weaknesses. However, by combining the ability to track responsibilities (the assignment notebook) with better organization of papers and possessions, students learn the lifelong skill of managing materials, an incredible time saver and a key to long-term success.

STRATEGY 1: MATERIAL ORGANIZATION — SUMMARY CHECKLIST

The checklist is a guide to help you progress through each step of teaching material organization to your child.

Set Up Assignment Notebook

❑ 1. Write subjects and dates for one month. Do not include subjects that rarely give homework (i.e., chorus or P.E.).

❑ 2. Make a section for extracurricular activities, such as sports, clubs, religious school, or chores.

❑ 3. Make a "Don't Forget" section to list supplies needed for homework, like textbooks.

❑ 4. Color code all information:
- **Red** = Test or quiz
- **Blue** = Long-term project
- **Black** = Nightly homework
- Green = Fun activities

❑ 5. Create and use a check/cross-check box.
- Check when the assignment is completed.

- Cross-check when an assignment is placed in the binder and put into the backpack.
❑ 6. Complete every box every day. Ask teachers to sign the assignment notebook. Older students will need to have it signed after each class, whereas the younger student with one class can have the assignment notebook signed at the end of the day. Parents should sign the assignment notebook when all homework is completed and packed.

Set Up Binder
❑ 1. Choose and set up a binder:
  - Traditional three-ring: Add folder pockets and supply pouch.
  - Accordion file: Label each subject, leave front pocket for homework and back pocket for blank paper.
  - Separate notebooks for each subject. Be sure folder pockets are included.
❑ 2. Check and reorganize weekly.

Set Up an Area for Other Materials
❑ Help the student develop a well-stocked, dedicated area for homework and a separate area for things needed each day (jacket, cell phone, wallet, etc.).

THINKING ORGANIZED HOMEWORK

Maintain a properly organized assignment notebook and binder system. Check each evening, and reward as appropriate, for the following:
- Assignment Notebook
  - Color coding is used.

- Items are listed in the "Don't Forget" section.
- Something is written in every subject.
- The check/cross-check is used.
- Extracurricular commitments are included.
- Binder Management
  - Papers are filed in the correct section.
  - Pockets are used for current work.
- Other Materials
  - Daily check-in and check-out is used.

Once your child has made progress in organizing school materials, you might consider helping him organize in other ways. Perhaps his room is disorganized. Or maybe the dash to sports practice is often a problem. See what systems you can develop together to handle these other aspects of material organization.

Strategy 2

Time Management

Time management is one of life's most important skills, and it often causes great difficulty for children as well as adults. The ability to fulfill obligations at work and home has much to do with the ability to manage time. Missed appointments, consistent tardiness, and a feeling of being constantly rushed are among the frustrations caused by poor time management.

As a student becomes conscious of time, it is easier for her to succeed in school and extracurricular activities. A student with executive function weaknesses frequently has difficulty managing time effectively. She may have trouble estimating how long an assignment will take and therefore experience frustration when she leaves too little time to complete a project. When given a task with multiple steps, the student may struggle to break the project down into manageable parts.

This is especially true with long-term assignments or tests. A disorganized student often feels that she has plenty of time to study, only to end up cramming the night before an exam. As a student moves through high school, she is required to complete more long-term projects as well as study for cumulative tests and quizzes. Poor time management can significantly affect a student's performance.

Sarah was starting seventh grade and expressed great anticipation about a science project requiring her to create an animal. Students were given three months to conduct their research, write a report, and create a 3D representation of a futuristic animal that could have evolved from an existing animal. Interim due dates were scheduled for the research and pre-writing portion of the project, but students were to plan and create the visual representation independently. Sarah met each of the interim due dates but believed that the visual representation and final written work would not take much time to complete. However, the weekend before the project was due, Sarah started getting nervous and began falling apart. Her mother had to cancel the family's weekend plans in order to help Sarah buy supplies and complete her project. It took two full days of constant effort on the part of both Sarah and her mother to complete the project. Due to her poor planning and the lack of time, the end result was not the masterpiece Sarah envisioned.

Fortunately, time management skills can be learned. Parents can help students become aware of time every day: how it is spent, how it is wasted, how it is planned, and how quickly it passes. Practicing the activities in this chapter — documenting time, estimating time, and breaking down long-term projects — will help your student become a better manager of her time and ultimately benefit the whole family.

GOALS

This strategy enhances the student's awareness of time and increases the ability to manage time appropriately.

1. *Awareness*: Increase the student's awareness of time and how it passes. You will use a time log to record time and encourage your student to wear a watch every day.

2. *Estimation*: Improve the student's ability to estimate time. You can practice guessing how long an activity will take and compare that to how long it actually took. This will help your student estimate time more accurately.

3. *Breaking down assignments*: Teach the student how to break long-term projects into meaningful parts. You will practice first with a fun activity (our example is a birthday party) and then with a research paper.

PREPARATION

Before beginning to teach your child the components of proper time management, you will need to collect the following supplies:

- A package of lined paper. This can be used for a time log (How Do I Spend My Time?) and to practice estimating time.
- A watch for your child.

- A kitchen timer.
- A monthly calendar.
- Red, blue, green, and black pens.

REVIEW

Before you begin to teach a new strategy, it is valuable to go back and review the most important parts of the preceding strategy. In Strategy 1, the main goal was proper use of the assignment notebook and binder. Because the materials were checked each night by the parent, this general review should start by praising the student for areas that she has consistently completed. Take the time to go through the week's assignments and correct any errors of filing, color coding, or omission. The goal is 100 percent completion of each step of the assignment notebook and binder. It is imperative that the student practice and learn these skills during the training sessions in order to exercise proper executive functioning skills independently. There is no reward for work that does not meet criteria.

Points or tokens can be awarded for these goals:
- Assignment Notebook
  - Color coding is used.
  - Items are listed in the "Don't Forget" section.
  - Something is written in every subject.
  - The check/cross-check is used.
  - Extracurricular commitments are included.
- Binder Management
  - Papers are filed in the correct section.
  - Pockets are used for current work.
- Other Materials

- Daily check-in and check-out is used.

When you have completed your review of Strategy 1, you can safely move on to teach the new material found in Strategy 2.

GOAL 1: AWARENESS

Time Log

Students often do not realize how much of each day is taken up by activities that they do not control. For example, going to school happens within a set time frame and can easily be documented. The trouble is managing time after school. When a student returns from school, she is asked to make good use of her time at home. However, a thirty-minute snack can easily turn into a three-hour break. Additionally, a student participating in an after-school activity rarely accounts for the time needed to get to and from that activity. Therefore, the student is left with less time to complete homework than originally planned.

Ask your child to record how she spends her time during a week. See table 2.1 for a sample log sheet. (You can download the sheets from www.thinkingorganized.com or make one yourself.) Documenting time in this way provides a visual representation of how much time is actually *not* available because it is taken up with school and other routine tasks.

When your student has completed one week of the time log, review it together. Look for the problem areas where time was mismanaged as well as areas when time was well used. For example, the student may recognize that when she comes home after school, it takes her a long time to start her homework. However, the day she went to the

© 2007, Rhona M. Gordon, Thinking Organized. All Rights Reserved. Duplication Prohibited.

Daytime	Monday	Tuesday	Wednesday	Thursday	Friday	Saturday	Sunday
7:00 AM	Get ready for school	Get ready for school	Get ready for school	Get ready for school	Get ready for school	Sleep late	Sleep late
7:30 AM	Go to school	Go to school	Go to school	Go to school	Go to school	Watch cartoons	pack bag
8:00 AM	Homeroom	Homeroom	Homeroom	Homeroom	Homeroom	Go out to breakfast	Drive to Grandma's
8:30 AM	Math	Math	Math	Math	Math	Shopping with Mom	Still in car
9:00 AM	Math	Math	Math	Math	Math	shopping	Breakfast at Grandmas
9:30 AM	Reading	Reading	Reading	Reading	Reading	shopping	Get ready for Church
10:00 AM	Reading	Reading	Reading	Reading	Reading	Unload cart	Go to Church
10:30 AM	Science	Science	Science	Science	Science	Get ready for Soccer	Church
11:00 AM	Science	Science	Science	Science	Science	Go to soccer game	Church
11:30 AM	Lunch	Lunch	Lunch	Lunch	Lunch	Soccer Game	Cookies and play
12:00 PM	PE	PE	PE	PE	PE	Soccer Game	Go home
12:30 PM	Spanish	Spanish	Spanish	Spanish	Spanish	Soccer Game	Eat Lunch
1:00 PM	Spanish	Spanish	Spanish	Spanish	Spanish	post-game Pizza	Clean room
1:30 PM	Leadership	Leadership	Leadership	Leadership	Leadership	post-game Pizza	Practice Piano
2:00 PM	Leadership	Leadership	Leadership	Leadership	Leadership	post-game Pizza	Work in yard

Table 2.1a **Sample Time Log**

© 2007, Rhona M. Gordon, Thinking Organized. All Rights Reserved. Duplication Prohibited.

Aft/Eve/Night	Monday	Tuesday	Wednesday	Thursday	Friday	Saturday	Sunday
2:30 PM	Go home from school.	Go home from school.	Go home from school.	Go home from school.	Go home from school.	Drive home from game	Work in yard.
3:00 PM	Snack	Play with friends	Go to Wendy's	Sell Candy for school.	Snack	Put away gear / shower	Drive to Library
3:30 PM	Eat & watch TV	Play with friends	Go to park.	Sell Candy w/ friend	Eat & watch TV	Watch TV	Research project
4:00 PM	Homework	Watch TV	Go to park	Play with friend	Homework	Watch TV	Research project
4:30 PM	Homework	Clean room	Homework	Play with friend	Homework	Call friend	Drive home
5:00 PM	Piano Lessons	Play computer	Homework	Watch TV	Piano Lessons	Play computer	Play with friends
5:30 PM	Piano	Play computer	Watch TV	practice piano	Piano	practice Piano	Play with friends
6:00 PM	Drive home	Homework	Watch TV	Fell asleep	Drive home	Watch TV	Help with Dinner
6:30 PM	Help with dinner	Eat dinner	Eat dinner	napped	Help with dinner	Watch TV	Eat dinner
7:00 PM	Eat dinner	Help clean up from dinner	Get ready / drive to basketball	Eat dinner	Eat dinner	Watch TV	Help clean up from dinner
7:30 PM	Take a bath	Play with sister	Bball practice	Help clean up from dinner	Take a bath	Go to babysit	Take a bath
8:00 PM	Play computer	Letter to Aunt Sue	Bball practice	Watch TV	Play computer	Babysit / TV	Watch TV
8:30 PM	Play computer	Read magazine	Go home / drive thru	Read with Mom	Play computer	Babysit / TV	Watch TV
9:00 PM	Read with sister	Watch TV	Take shower	Take a bath	Play with sister	Babysit / TV	Read (homework)
9:30 PM	Pack backpack	Take a bath	Read	Organize for tomorrow	Study / pack backpack	Babysit / TV	Read (homework)
10:00 PM	Go to bed	Go to bed	Go to bed	Go to bed	Go to bed	Babysit / TV	Go to bed

Table 2.1b **Sample Time Log (continued)**

library after school, she finished her work and had free time in the evening.

It is often useful to have a student compare her log sheet with one completed by the parent. Judging someone else's use of time gives another perspective on time management and increases confidence in mastering this skill. Estimating and calculating time for family activities such as meal times, parties, or vacations teaches students that effective time management is important in all aspects of life — not just in schoolwork.

Wearing a Watch

Another part of building time awareness is encouraging the child to use a watch. Choose a watch that your child will enjoy wearing and remind her to wear it daily. Ask your child questions about time to increase her awareness. For example, a mother could ask, "What time is it now, and what time do we need to leave for soccer practice?" By reminding her child to check the time regularly, she is increasing the student's awareness of time and its passing.

Older students often resist wearing a watch, saying that their cell phone displays the time. However, most schools do not allow cell phones to be on during the day, making a wristwatch the fastest and most efficient way to find the time. If your student strongly resists wearing a watch, encourage her to use the clocks at school and her cell phone at all other times. A student can use the cell phone not only to check the time, but also to set automatic reminders.

GOAL 2: ESTIMATION

Guess / Actual Time Sheet

The guess/actual time sheet helps the student learn to manage time. Instruct the student to list her assignments. Because the assignments are listed in the assignment notebook, the student can simply write the subject area, like "math" or "science" on the guess/actual time sheet. Table 2.2 on the following page provides a sample.

Next, the student should guess how long an assignment will take. This should be done for each subject, including work on a long-term project or studying for a test. The student should be told that she is not racing the clock but rather using the clock to become better at gauging time. Table 2.3 on the following page provides a sample.

Of course, the next step is to have the student do her homework, recording the actual time as she does it. After the student has her materials ready, she should make a note of the time. When she has completed the work, she should record the actual time it took to finish the assignment. If the student becomes distracted with timing her work, then an outside person in a different room can be the timer. Once the actual time is recorded, writing a quick explanatory note on the guess/actual time sheet will help a student plan better in the future. Table 2.4 on the following page provides a sample.

From table 2.4, one can see that the student consistently underestimated how much time her homework would take. When she attempts this task again, she will need to add extra time for each assignment.

Many students report that they cannot keep time because they just like to start their homework and continue until it is completed. Others argue they do not have "time" to complete the guess/actual time sheet. Don't be fooled by these excuses — neither one is acceptable. A student must time all work while participating in the Thinking Organized program. The

© 2007, Rhona M. Gordon, Thinking Organized. All Rights Reserved. Duplication Prohibited.

Activity	Guess Time	Actual Time
Math		
Science		
Reading		

Table 2.2 **Guess / Actual Time Sheet**

Activity	Guess Time	Actual Time
Math	30 minutes	
Science	10 minutes	
Reading	20 minutes	

Table 2.3 **Guess / Actual Time Sheet with Estimates**

Activity	Guess Time	Actual Time
Math	30 minutes	45 minutes
Science	10 minutes	30 minutes
Reading	20 minutes	55 minutes

Table 2.4 **Guess / Actual Time Sheet with Estimates and Actuals**

truth is that estimating the timing of a project helps a student get started and limits procrastination of difficult tasks. Once the clock is set, the student tends to start her work without further delay.

It's important to note that students sometimes become anxious when they know they are being timed and rush through their work. If this is the case, first practice using the guess/actual time sheets with an activity that is fun or involves other family members.

This exercise presents a good opportunity to talk with your child about prioritizing. Not all students begin their homework in the same way. Some students prefer to tackle the most challenging piece of homework first to get it completed while they are most alert. Others like to begin with a quick, fifteen-minute worksheet in order to feel a sense of accomplishment. The danger in beginning with the easiest tasks is the opportunity it presents for procrastination; the longer the larger task is undone, the greater the possibility that it will not be completed. For a student who likes to begin with something easy, have her tackle the first portion of a more difficult assignment immediately after completing a quick worksheet. Sandwiching harder assignments or even parts of assignments in between easier tasks can help the student complete the more challenging assignments without feeling overwhelmed. Help your student decide the order of priority according to what works best for her.

Practice

It's a good idea to practice using the guess/actual time sheets for a variety of activities. This will help the student become more aware of time and realize that time is important at home and in school. Choose one or all of the activities for practicing

© 2007, Rhona M. Gordon, Thinking Organized. All Rights Reserved. Duplication Prohibited.

Activity	Guess Time	Actual Time
Grocery shopping	45 minutes	60 minutes
Putting away groceries	20 minutes	10 minutes
Cooking dinner	30 minutes	45 minutes

Table 2.5 **Guess / Actual Time Sheet for Parent Activities**

guess/actual time, which you will find following the Strategy 2 checklist. Parents can model the recording of time by using a guess/actual time sheet for their own activities.

In the example found in table 2.5, the parent underestimated two activities but overestimated the third. It is important to point out to your child that even a weekly task can be difficult to estimate. Therefore a parent, just like a child, needs to practice estimating time in order to become accurate.

Encourage the student to complete several guess/actual time sheets during the week. Younger children may need more time and direction to complete this task. As the student becomes proficient at guessing time, she can incorporate the guess/actual time into her assignment notebook. Add a box in the lower left corner and one in the lower right corner of each subject area. The student should mark her guess time in the box on the left and the actual time on the right.

GOAL 3: BREAKING DOWN ASSIGNMENTS

One of the most important aspects of time management is learning to divide a large project into specific tasks. When the disorganized thinker is given a long-term assignment such as a research project, the response is either panic or procrastination. However, by practicing the time management skill of breaking a long-term assignment into smaller, more manageable goals, you can show your child that even a large task can be completed in advance of the deadline without struggling, tears, or last minute panic.

Start by explaining that it does not matter whether large tasks are for school or fun, they still need to be broken down into smaller sections in order to be accomplished. A great example is to plan a pretend (or real) birthday party. If you are having a party you first have to choose a date, then make a list of things to do, and when you will do them. Use a calendar to demonstrate that if you want to know how many people are coming at least one week before the party, you will need to send the invitations three weeks before. That means the guest list will need to be finalized four weeks before the party date. See table 2.6 for a sample breakdown of birthday party preparations.

Planning and completing a large school assignment is accomplished in the same way as planning a birthday party. It is important to map out a schedule as soon as a large project is given. Procrastination can lead to disaster — the due date that seemed so far away creeps up quickly, and all of a sudden time is limited. Scheduling a long-term assignment allows for some of life's unforeseen obstacles, such as a visit from an old friend, a bout with the flu, or the library being closed on the day scheduled for research. It is important to plan to use weekends for long-term projects as weekdays quickly become filled with homework and extracurricular activities.

© 2007, Rhona M. Gordon, Thinking Organized. All Rights Reserved. Duplication Prohibited.

JOHN'S BIRTHDAY PARTY — JUNE 30TH	
Jobs to accomplish *before* RSVPs (RSVP date of June 21st)	
Finalize guest list	May 30
Buy invitations	June 2
Send invitations	June 7
Plan entertainment	June 15
Jobs to accomplish *after* RSVPs	
Buy favors	June 22
Plan menu	June 23
Buy food / start cooking	June 25 – June 29
Pick up ice cream cake	June 29
Pick up balloons	June 30

Table 2.6 **Breakdown of a Large Project**

Research Paper

When mapping out a research paper, the student should write deadlines on a calendar for the seven essential steps in breaking down the assignment. (See Strategy 6 for more in-depth information about writing a research paper.)

1. *Choosing a topic*: This should be done within the first three to five days of receiving the project, as this affects all subsequent work. To help a student choose a topic, encourage her to ask questions such as: What is the goal for this project? What exactly should be researched? Break the project down into questions that can be answered, and use the instruction sheet to determine how many and what kind of sources are needed.

2. *Research*: If the project requires only online sources, there is no need to allot time for the library. However, if other documents must be used or obtained, then start by mapping time to spend one or two sessions at the library looking for books and articles. More complicated assignments will need further time at the library. Remember to mark on your calendar days that the library may be closed or when family plans will interfere.

3. *Note-taking*: Enough time needs to be added to the schedule to not only gather research material, but to carefully read and understand the information, and then to take notes on it in the student's own words.

4. *Plan to write*: The disorganized student needs to be reminded to write according to a formal structure. Before beginning to write, encourage the student to make bullet points, a formal outline, or a web to organize her ideas.

5. *Writing*: When scheduling writing time, remember to build in extra days for revising and editing.
6. *Buddy check*: Have a parent, teacher, or trusted friend read the paper to check for errors or something that does not make sense.
7. *Final check*: This is the final check for spelling, punctuation, grammar, and neatness. Plan to have this done on the Sunday before the paper is due. Although this due date may seem early, remember that nightly homework will still be assigned during the week. Therefore, weekends are the optimal time to complete long-term projects.

Use a Calendar

Another important strategy for students is to list assignments and activities on a monthly calendar. This is an excellent way to help them learn to break down assignments and manage their time. Utilize the color-coding system introduced in Strategy 1 to list tests, projects, and extracurricular plans. All long-term assignments, even tests, should be broken down in either the assignment notebook or on a monthly calendar. Remember that it is not enough for the student to write "study." Insist on specifics, such as "reread chapter 4 and answer questions," or "make note cards." Writing down specific short-term goals helps a student better prepare for upcoming tests and assignments and lets her see at a glance that she has time to complete her assignments and still has time for fun.

Figure 2.1 illustrates how a student can list specific details needed to complete work on a monthly calendar. It is also acceptable to list individual tasks related to studying and long-term projects in the assignment notebook. Some students prefer this method.

© 2007, Rhona M. Gordon, Thinking Organized. All Rights Reserved. Duplication Prohibited.

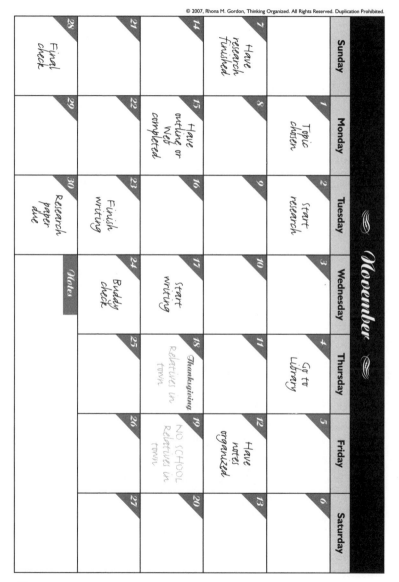

Figure 2.1 **Sample Monthly Calendar with Planned Project**

STRATEGY 2: TIME MANAGEMENT
SUMMARY CHECKLIST

The checklist is a guide to help you progress through each step of teaching time management to your child.

❑ 1. Use a time log to demonstrate how time is spent and wasted.

❑ 2. Use the guess/actual time sheets to practice estimating time to complete homework and other activities. Talk about prioritizing homework and activities.

❑ 3. Wear a watch.

❑ 4. Demonstrate how long-term projects can be broken down into manageable parts, and list exact tasks in the assignment notebook.

❑ 5. Practice completing a monthly calendar with the color patterns used in the assignment notebook:
- **Red** = Test or quiz
- **Blue** = Long-term project
- **Black** = Nightly homework
- **Green** = Fun activities

THINKING ORGANIZED HOMEWORK

The homework is to help the student continue to establish habits for effective time management. Check periodically and reward as appropriate, for the following:

1. Use of time log.
2. Continued use and practice with guess/actual time sheets. (Use the fun activities that follow for additional practice.)
3. Use of monthly calendar with plenty of entries.
4. A watch is being worn each day.

FUN ACTIVITIES FOR GUESS/ACTUAL TIME PRACTICE

Sports Practice
- How much time do you need to put your sports clothing on and get your equipment together?
- How long does it take to drive to practice?
- How much time is spent at practice?
- How long does it take to get home?
- What do you do when you get home? Shower? Put away gear? Relax? How much time is spent on these activities?

Play Date
- How much time will you spend calling to organize time and place?
- How much time will it take to prepare activities for the play date?
- How much time will be spent playing?
- How much time will it take to clean up and say goodbye?

Dinner
Parents and kids can do this one together.
- How long does it take to prepare and serve dinner, even if you are not the one doing it? Include setting the table, getting everyone a drink, and serving the food.
- How long does it take to eat dinner?
- How long does it take to clean up from dinner?

The Family Vacation
Parents and kids can do this one together.

- How much time is spent choosing a place and picking the activities?
- How much time is spent getting the clothing together, packing medicines, music, books, and so forth?
- How much time is spent preparing the house, including making arrangements for pets and mail pick-up?
- What is the travel time to the destination?
- What is the time to be spent at the destination?
- How long will it take to get home from the destination?
- How much time will it take to unpack, put away souvenirs, give travel gifts, go through the mail, and check e-mail after returning home?

Even children who appear to be ideal students can benefit from better time management skills. Kimberly was one of those students. She documented assignments with bright colors, came to class with all of her books, and almost always turned in nightly homework. However, Kimberly had great difficulty completing long-term projects. She did not know how to break down large assignments or where to begin. Frequently she got involved with the individual details of her goal and lost sight of the need to finish on time. For example, when working on a research presentation, Kimberly became so engrossed in choosing the right colors for the visual portion that she ran out of time to research her report. She had to stay up to the wee hours of the morning in order to complete the paper on time. The quality of her written work suffered as a result of her poor planning; her grade reflected this.

Kimberly's mother recognized that better time management would help improve her daughter's grades and reduce her stress level. Kimberly and her mother began

Toward Independence!

A wonderful way to model effective use of time is to schedule a day each week to work on the family's monthly calendar. This can involve the whole family or just be between a parent and child. Each person takes a turn to schedule in obligations, extracurricular activities, and other fun events. The student learns that even adults must plan ahead in order to manage time effectively. Reinforcing this behavior at an adult level enables the student to utilize the same strategy within her own sphere.

practicing strategies from the Thinking Organized program, such as estimating time for routine tasks and logging time to identify how it was being spent. Kimberly learned that color coding is only effective if used in a limited, systematic way. She began to create outlines to identify main ideas and supporting details and had fun learning new strategies to secure information into memory. Kimberly's mother helped her break down long-term projects into manageable goals, assign interim deadlines for each one, and revise the schedule as needed. Kimberly now recognizes that planning her time effectively is the best way to get good grades. Strategy 2 can help your child achieve the same results.

Strategy 3

Learning Styles & Studying

*S*tudying is a skill that can be taught. Learning how to study helps students complete tasks effectively and efficiently. Both knowing one's own learning style and knowing effective strategies for studying contribute to developing strong executive functioning skills.

This chapter deals with two areas of studying. One is to help the student find the best way to learn new material, his specific studying style. The second part of the chapter helps the student understand that spending an inordinate amount of time may not be the surest path to success. It is important to learn effective studying strategies that will maximize his efforts.

Sometimes students are asked to learn material a certain way. Billy's teacher taught multiplication tables visually, which seemed to work for most of the class. The students practiced by taking timed tests and referring to a key on their desk. However, Billy could not memorize his multiplication tables this way. He became frustrated because no matter how many tests he attempted, he never finished within the allotted time period. Billy's teacher helped him create an alternative way to study, using his love of music. She provided CDs that set each group of multiplication tables to a catchy song. Billy walked around with his headphones on for hours each day, singing along with the CD. The auditory method of learning worked for Billy; and once he realized this, he was able to apply the same technique to other subjects, lessening his frustration and maximizing his studying time and efforts.

GOALS

Learning how to study can save students time and improve their performance.

1. *Learning style:* Help the student discover more about his individual learning style and preferences.
2. *New strategies:* Incorporate some new strategies that will appeal to his style of learning.
3. *Study habits and techniques:* Practice good studying habits every day to ensure that work is current and no materials are missing. Implement specific techniques to help a student study for a test or exam.

PREPARATION

It will be helpful to have these supplies handy to teach your child effective studying techniques:

1. *Non-fiction text*: You will need a social studies or science textbook, or any non-fiction text, that is not too difficult for your child to read and understand. This will be helpful in demonstrating that studying begins when the student first reads text material.
2. *A dedicated study area*: You may decide to include gum, a water bottle, or a squishy ball as focus points to maintain concentration. Sometimes having a physical manipulative helps the student stay focused on his work rather than searching for a distraction in the environment.

REVIEW

Make sure the student is consistently completing the assignment notebook and the guess/actual time sheet. It is important to be strict with the rules to help the student properly internalize material and time organization.

Some students catch on quickly and recognize the benefits of using the information presented in the first two strategies. However, most students have a harder time habitualizing these skills. Don't despair; remain consistent in your demands and the structure provided for the student. This is crucial for organizational success.

To reinforce lessons in material and time management, additional sessions may be warranted. For extra practice with time management, use a daily and a monthly calendar for students to assign and plot hypothetical long-term projects.

Points or tokens can be awarded for the following:
- Assignment Notebook
  - Color coding is used.
  - Items are listed in the "Don't Forget" section.
  - Something is written in every subject.
  - The check/cross-check is used.
  - Extracurricular commitments are included.
- Binder Management
  - Papers are filed in the correct section.
  - Pockets are used for current work.
- Other Materials
  - Daily check-in and check-out is used.
- Time Management
  - Use of time log.
  - Practice with guess/actual time sheets.
  - Monthly calendar is marked with long-term assignments.
  - The student is wearing a watch.

When you have completed your review of Strategies 1 and 2, you can safely move on to teaching Strategy 3.

GOAL 1: LEARNING STYLE

Every person prefers a certain method for learning new material. Some like to hear the information they have to remember while others would rather read it. Successful students incorporate a variety of strategies for effective learning. The predominant learning styles are visual, auditory, and kinesthetic. Using more than one style often helps students become further engaged in the process of studying.

The visual learner relies mostly on his sense of sight.

For example, he would prefer to read new information rather than listen to a lecture. In a classroom setting, a visual learner benefits from taking careful notes and connecting ideas with colors and images.

An auditory student learns mostly by listening and speaking. In a lecture, the auditory learner prefers to concentrate on what is being said, rather than taking notes. For this type of learner, verbally discussing material will help him better understand connections and secure information into memory.

A kinesthetic learner likes to touch things and move around. It is hard for a student to use only a kinesthetic approach because in a traditional academic setting, children are required to sit in their seats. Kinesthetic learning does take place in the classroom when a student is asked to role-play a historical time period or perform a science experiment. In school, the early grades incorporate a great deal of movement, which benefits the kinesthetic student. In later grades, the use of kinesthetic learning in the classroom decreases. Therefore, it is important that the student who prefers the kinesthetic approach practices using other learning styles. One way a kinesthetic learner can concentrate in a lecture is by taking notes with pictures or using different colors to stay engaged with the material.

Most people utilize more than one learning modality. For example, in a lecture a student is required to listen and take notes, using both the auditory and visual channels. When young children learn the alphabet, they likely use the auditory technique of listening and singing the alphabet song. They also use visual learning by looking at alphabet books. Kinesthetic learners form letters in the sand or move magnets on the refrigerator. Our work has found that when students utilize more than one modality, they are more likely to learn and retain the information.

For example, visual learners have the advantage of being able to take notes in a classroom. However, it would be beneficial for visual learners to try listening in a study group for information that they may have missed in the lecture. Auditory learners would also benefit from a study group because taking notes may be difficult for them to do while listening. Because the academic world is primarily visual, auditory learners will need to practice visual strategies such as note-taking to help them remember information. Students who use a kinesthetic approach need to stay active while learning by writing notes or highlighting material. When students use a combination of strategies, they learn information more effectively and efficiently.

Learning Styles Assessment Questionnaire
No one is purely a visual, auditory, or kinesthetic learner. A student who prefers auditory learning is still likely to use several visual and kinesthetic techniques. The following questions should help your student begin to think about the way he learns information. Read each question carefully with your child and then decide together which answer best describes him.

Interpret Your Results!
- If most of the responses are ones, your student is most likely a *visual learner*.
- If most of the responses are twos, your student is most likely an *auditory learner*.
- If most of the responses are threes, your student is most likely a *kinesthetic learner*.

© 2007, Rhona M. Gordon, Thinking Organized. All Rights Reserved. Duplication Prohibited.

Question	Answer One	Answer Two	Answer Three
When learning something new in science, do you prefer to:	read the textbook	listen to an explanation	complete an experiment in the science lab
When studying for a spelling test, do you:	try to picture the word in your mind	recite the letters out loud or in your head	write the word to see if it "feels" right
Do you prefer stories with:	good descriptions, so you can picture the scene	good dialogue, so you can understand what is happening between the characters	lots of action, because it is hard to sit still and read
How do you stay focused when listening to a long lecture?	take notes	take no notes but listen closely	take sporadic notes, even if you choose not to use them later
If you are trying to concentrate, do you get distracted by:	clutter or movement nearby	sounds and noises, either too quiet or too loud	activity happening around you
If packing gear for a soccer game (or any extracurricular activity) do you:	make a list in your head or on paper	wait for your mother to call out what you need	just start packing without thinking about it first
When you have a problem, do you:	organize your thoughts with lists	talk to yourself or a friend	engage in physical activity, like walking around or jogging
When talking to a friend, do you:	like to meet the person face-to-face	prefer to talk on the phone	walk or move around as you talk
If you run into someone you have only met once before, you are most likely to remember:	his face or how he looked	his name or the sound of his voice	his mannerisms or hand motions

Table 3.1 **Learning Styles Assessment Questionnaire**

GOAL 2: NEW STRATEGIES

Help your child incorporate some new studying strategies that may be helpful for his learning style. Finding which techniques work best will encourage your student to develop his own personal method of studying. Knowing *how* to learn will help him on the road to Thinking Organized.

Strategies for Visual Learners:
- Draw charts, tables, graphs, diagrams, pictures.
- Use Post-it Notes.
- Use color to highlight important points in a text.
- Make lists and categorize information.
- Use the computer, digital camera, or camcorder to make notes or explanations of material.
- Practice visualizing information to be memorized.

Strategies for Auditory Learners
- Verbalization
  - Repeat words aloud.
  - Read text out loud.
  - After reading, summarize key points out loud.
  - Create musical jingles to aid memorization.
  - Use verbal analogies and stories to remember key points.
  - Make speeches and presentations.
- Record and Play Back
  - Tape record lectures and listen to them as soon as possible after class.
  - Tape record notes after each class and listen to them later.
  - Listen to difficult material again and again, while traveling, jogging, or doing chores.

- Involve Others
  - Listen and discuss subject materials with others.
  - Try to teach a younger sibling or explain material to a classmate, parent, even a pet!
  - Participate in class discussions as much as possible.
  - Organize a study group, where material is discussed orally.
  - Ask a lot of questions.

Strategies for Kinesthetic Learners
- Keep a stress ball close by to help stay focused.
- Touch each finger of your hand to remember five items, both hands for ten items.
- Take frequent study breaks to move around.
- Use pictures or drawings to help while taking notes in class.
- Use movement while studying (for example: reading while on an exercise bike, molding a piece of clay while learning a new concept, tossing a ball in the air while memorizing, reciting spelling words while riding a bike around the block, jumping rope while repeating math facts).
- Try working in different positions, like standing up.
- Chew gum while studying.
- Highlight while reading.

GOAL 3: STUDY HABITS AND TECHNIQUES

Kevin spent a lot of time studying. Every day after school, he would lock himself in his room for hours at a time. However, he did not get the grades he expected on tests and came to me for help. Kevin reported that he had recently spent five hours studying for a history test. He memorized dates and facts and thought he knew the information thoroughly. However, the test required Kevin to write an essay for which he was unprepared. He studied for a multiple choice type test, rather than spending time integrating the material for an essay. For the next test, Kevin and I spent time verbally discussing the material, writing webs to show connections, and brainstorming for possible essay questions. He came out of the test with a smile on his face, confident that he had prepared efficiently.

Bright students frequently do not learn and practice effective studying skills in elementary school. When learning comes easily, these students do not feel they need to do anything extra. As academic material becomes more difficult, they sometimes are caught without the proper skills to learn efficiently. Instituting effective studying strategies is helpful to any student, but the earlier they are taught, the more easily they become habit.

Getting Ready to Study

The first thing to do is discuss where a student should study. Some students need complete silence, while others need noise. Some like to sit straight up at a desk, while others prefer to recline on a bed or the floor. Although the bedroom works well for many children, some have difficulty staying alert in the same room where they sleep or they have trouble concentrating when surrounded by playthings. Help the student determine the optimum place for effective studying.

Often parents feel that the child will be more productive in a quiet room, but this is not always the case. If noise is needed, be sure the student understands that a television or rap music is too distracting. Noise means background noise that masks other sounds, such as classical music or white noise. Alternatively, sitting in or near the kitchen might provide enough background noise to keep the child engaged. Another benefit to being near a parent while working is that the parent can keep the student on task with gentle reminders. Some older students report that the house is too distracting and have greater success studying at the library or a quiet corner of a coffee shop.

For students who have difficulty getting started or staying focused, chewing gum can be very helpful. Other ideas are to keep a water bottle nearby or use a squishy ball to keep hands occupied while reading.

Everyday Studying

Studying begins when a student first reads the material. Therefore, practice these active reading strategies to further engage your child with the text as he is reading. The more a student interacts with the material, the more likely he is to remember it.

1. ***Titles, headlines, and pictures***: Before reading, look at titles, headlines, and pictures. Everyone knows this strategy, yet few people use it regularly. It only takes a student a few minutes to get a general overview of the chapter, but this tool can be invaluable in sorting main ideas from details.

2. ***Read before highlighting***: Next, read a paragraph in its entirety before highlighting or taking notes. If the student is highlighting in the book, ask him to highlight two or three details that support the bolded headlines. Writing a few key words on the side of the paragraph will help jog his memory when reviewing the information for an exam. Another way to remember what

was read is by taking notes either in a notebook or on the computer.

3. ***Keep track of questions***: If the student has a question while reading, encourage him to mark it with a large red question mark or by using a Post-it Note so that he can ask a teacher or research it on his own at a later date.

4. ***Follow through***: Continue with each paragraph until the assignment is completed. Although the student may complain that this takes longer than just reading, he soon learns that this process saves him studying time before an exam.

It is especially important for the disorganized student to keep up with homework and daily assignments. If he stays current with his work, he will be more likely to notice material that he is missing or identify questions he has about the subject matter. This makes studying for a test more systematic and orderly. See Strategy 5 for further discussion on note-taking for reading comprehension.

Studying for a Test

1. ***Start with good study habits***: To really make studying easy, the student should review his class notes on a weekly basis. All he has to do is read them over at the end of the week and clarify any confusing information. This ten-minute exercise will help him become familiar with the material and make studying for the test much easier.

2. ***Study in advance***: Start studying for a test *five* days in advance and for a quiz, *three* days.

3. ***Schedule study time***: Schedule your student's studying time on a daily calendar and write down what will be

studied each night. It is not good enough to write the word "study" in his assignment notebook. Divide the material into manageable parts so that he will have a specific amount of material to cover each night. Plan to finish studying all the material at least two days before the test, so that the night before the test can be devoted to problem areas and a general review.

4. *Collect information*: Help your student collect all information from class notes, handouts, textbook, quizzes, and previous tests. If his notes are not complete or legible, he should copy them from a friend or ask to borrow the teacher's notes. When he starts far enough ahead of time to prepare for an exam, he has the time to see what material is missing or confusing. Then he has a chance to remedy the situation. Remember, if he only has 70 percent of the information to study, he can only answer 70 percent of the questions!

5. *Questions*: Help your child prepare a sheet of questions to ask the teacher or a classmate two days before the exam. If he keeps the sheet with him as he begins studying, his questions will be ready for the teacher. Also, as he becomes more familiar with the material, he may answer his own questions.

6. *Create a study guide*: Using a class outline or an outline from the textbook as the basis, the student should create a comprehensive study guide. Adding notes from other sources will expand the outline. As the student writes the study guide, he is already putting small chunks of information systematically into his brain. This makes retrieval of information much easier. A kinesthetic or auditory learner can talk out loud as he

creates his outline.

Add additional information in different colors. For example, if he adds to class notes written in black ink, use green to signify that material is being added from the textbook and blue to show information added from handouts. This allows him to refer back to the source if there is a question he wants to clarify.

Your student will know about 80 percent of the material when he has finished creating a comprehensive study guide! The remaining 20 percent of the material can be learned using flash cards, mind maps, timelines, and other memory techniques. Memory skills are discussed more extensively in Strategy 4.

7. *Integrate the information*: This may be the hardest task of all. The student needs to determine why the information is important and how one piece relates to another. Encourage your student to discuss this with other students, especially if he has a hard time understanding the main points and how they relate to the topic he is studying.

8. *Prepare for an essay question*: On an essay question, the student must know three to five points about a subject area. Help your child write down how each point he will make relates to the main topic. He should provide an example from the material to support each statement. More information on preparing for essay questions can be found in Strategy 6.

9. *Form a study group*: In middle school and high school, it is often a good idea to study with others. Although some parents feel that actual work does not take place, study groups offer the opportunity to make sure each student understands the material and has

studied in a comprehensive manner. The students should use the study session to quiz each other on important information and create outlines for possible essay questions. Reward the scholars with a pizza or an ice cream party *after* the studying is done.

10. **The night before**: The night before the exam should be for a general review and to go over the more difficult pieces of the material. Any information that continues to be difficult to memorize should be reviewed once before the child goes to sleep and then again on the way to the test.

Be flexible. Encourage the student to be flexible in his approach to studying. Not every subject can be learned in the same manner. Studying for a math test involves practicing problems while studying for history requires reading and analysis. Therefore, the student's most comfortable way of studying may not be the best method for learning the material. The student who is flexible in his approach to studying and willing to practice different strategies will lessen his frustration and learn material more easily.

STRATEGY 3: **LEARNING STYLES AND STUDYING SUMMARY CHECKLIST**

The checklist is a guide to help you progress through each step of teaching learning styles and studying to your child.

❑ 1. Help the student assess his own learning style by answering the questions within the chapter.

❑ 2. Encourage the student to try studying techniques that involve each of the following three learning styles:
   • Visual: Flash cards, diagrams, outlines.

- Auditory: Tapes, CDs, or oral recitations.
- Kinesthetic: Physical motion, such as walking, chewing gum, or squeezing a stress ball.

❑ 3. Help the student set up a dedicated study area, stock it with supplies, and choose tools to encourage focus (gum, stress balls, water bottles, and so forth).

❑ 4. Explain that studying begins when the student first reads the text. Use a social studies or science text to show the student how to read actively, using titles, bolded words, pictures, captions, and bullets to discuss main idea and supporting details.

❑ 5. Discuss effective methods of studying for a quiz or test.

THINKING ORGANIZED HOMEWORK

1. Try at least two new studying techniques that appeal to the student's individual learning style.
2. Practice doing homework in the dedicated location and utilize some of the studying techniques for tests.

In today's fast-changing society, knowing how to learn will always be an essential tool for success. Today's students cannot imagine life without computers, although not so long ago most offices used typewriters. A whole generation of adults had to learn about computers to keep up with the times. Who knows what new technologies or systems the workers of tomorrow will be required to learn? Learning how to integrate various strategies that work well for the individual develops a flexibility that will be a skill to be exercised throughout life.

Toward Independence!

*W*hen a student is beginning the Thinking Organized program, he will need a great deal of assistance in creating a study plan. The parent will help him dedicate enough time for studying on a monthly calendar and break down "studying for a test" into specific tasks such as "make flashcards." Furthermore, the parent will demonstrate how studying for an essay test differs from a factual multiple choice test.

As the student routinizes effective studying habits, the parent can monitor the studying process less closely. If the student has an appropriate studying plan with specific tasks scheduled, then a brief "check-in" may be all that is required. When test grades improve, the student's confidence in his ability to study is bolstered and he becomes motivated to continue the methods independently.

Strategy 4

Memory Strategies

*I*n order to explain memory strategies to students, it is helpful to try this visualization exercise. Imagine that you have a great, big toy box filled with one hundred wonderful toys of all sizes and shapes. Your task is to quickly find the small red car in the toy box. Now imagine how much easier it would be to find the car if those toys had originally been placed into boxes by categories, so there would be one box for blocks, one for the large toys, and maybe even one for little cars. This is our goal for developing systems to store information in the brain.

Linda's memory weaknesses were noticed when she started elementary school. She struggled to memorize math facts and spelling words. Her writing was frequently vague and off topic, as she sometimes forgot the prompt while writing. Linda's mom noticed these difficulties and worked to teach Linda some additional memory strategies. They began practicing memory games all the time — in the car, parking lot, and grocery store. One game they played started by asking Linda to retrieve five items from the produce section, gradually increasing the number of items to be remembered. Another strategy they practiced was making index cards for Linda's spelling words, using color coding and pictures. Gradually, Linda's ability to retain information in memory improved and she gained confidence in her ability to perform well in school.

Students are required to memorize information from a variety of subjects over many years. This presents a considerable problem for the student who has difficulty organizing information in her brain. Additionally, memorizing information that one understands is easier than remembering something that is not understood or of little interest. Often, the disorganized learner tries to cram information into memory the night before an exam. Therefore, this strategy is devoted to expanding memory by exploring a variety of ways to put information into the brain so that it can be easily retrieved.

GOAL

The main goal for this strategy is to improve memory.
- *Understanding memory*: The student will learn different ways to store information in memory.
- *Practicing memory strategies*: The student will practice various strategies to store information for more effective retrieval.

PREPARATION

Only one item is needed to practice memory strategies: a memory game. You may choose a deck of cards, several small objects, or you can purchase a memory game.

REVIEW

By Strategy 4, the student knows to have the assignment notebook, binder, and guess/actual time sheets ready for review. Remember to reward consistent use of the systems that were established in Strategies 1-3.

If a student is struggling with one of the goals, stop and try to get to the root of the problem. For example, some students do not like putting their guess/actual times on a separate sheet. After the student understands the principle of the timing, she can be taught to create two boxes in each subject of her assignment notebook. The guessed time should go in the left box and the actual time should be placed in the right. Putting all work on one page is very helpful for the student who has difficulty with managing papers.

Discuss how last chapter's studying techniques were used during the week. Encourage the student to keep trying new techniques when studying and remind her that the more she interacts with the material, the easier it will be to learn and retain it.

Points or tokens can be awarded for the following:
- Assignment Notebook
  - Color coding is used.
  - Items are listed in the "Don't Forget" section.
  - Something is written in every subject.

- • The check/cross-check is used.
- • Extracurricular commitments are included.
- • Binder Management
  - • Papers are filed in the correct section.
  - • Pockets are used for current work.
- • Other Materials
  - • Daily check-in and check-out location is used.
- • Time Management
  - • Guess/actual time sheet is used.
  - • Monthly calendar has color-coded entries.
  - • The student is wearing a watch.
- • Learning Strategies
  - • The student has tried a new study technique.

GOAL 1: UNDERSTANDING MEMORY

This strategy is devoted to exploring ways to put information into the brain so that it can be easily retrieved. To do this, the student should be taught to consider the entire body of information to be learned as the main idea and then concentrate on more specific units of information, or the details. As the student studies and learns detailed information, she should periodically stop and consider how the details relate to the main idea. For example, a disorganized student studying Dr. Martin Luther King may become so entrenched in the details of Dr. King's life that she forgets to relate the events of Dr. King's life to the main idea — Dr. King's role in America's civil rights movement.

It is helpful if the student practices linking specific information to the whole using various methods. A primarily visual learner could make flash cards, mind maps, or large poster boards to link the details to the main idea. The auditory learner may want to record the information on a headset and listen to it numerous times. A kinesthetic learner will find it helpful to incorporate movement in order to actively engage the whole body in the memorization process. No matter which studying methods are used, every student must save time to "over learn" the material; that is, to review it again and again, even when she feels she knows it well. The additional repetition will help the student secure information in long-term memory for easier retrieval in the future.

Giving labels to the different types of memory empowers the student and demystifies the learning process. Let's take a quick look at the three types of memory:

1. ***Short-term memory***: This allows the individual to remember information for only a short period of time. The amount that can be stored in short-term memory is limited. Information put into short-term memory needs to be used right away or put into long-term memory to prevent forgetting it. A good example is a seven-digit phone number. You might look it up, repeat it until you dial the number, and then forget it. From an academic perspective, when information is crammed into short-term memory for a test, the chances are pretty high that the information will not be retained in long-term memory.

2. ***Long-term memory***: This is where information is stored and readily retrieved at a later time, such as remembering your own address and phone number. For example, when your phone number changes, you tend to recall the old number until the new number

replaces it in long-term memory. Long-term memory is the one we will stress in this strategy. Information needs to be secured in long-term memory for effective and efficient retrieval.

3. *Active working memory*: This allows one to hold information in the mind while developing an idea, clarifying information, answering a question, or completing a multi-step task. If one forgets a single part of an assignment or loses track of the process, it will be difficult to complete the assignment accurately.

GOAL 2: PRACTICING MEMORY STRATEGIES

We'll briefly examine seven strategies here for your student to practice.

1. *Visualizing information*: To use this strategy, the student creates a visual image of the material to be remembered. This is a very effective technique, especially when used in combination with other strategies, such as chunking or mnemonics. Suppose your student is studying the geography of the United States. The student could visualize that the state of Florida looks like a boot at the bottom right of the map. (See figure 4.1 on the next page.) By remembering the picture, a student can easily recreate Florida's position on the U.S. map. Visualization is a critical memory strategy. Being able to see a mental picture helps the student remember information, retrieve it, and describe it effectively.

© 2007, Rhona M. Gordon, Thinking Organized. All Rights Reserved. Duplication Prohibited.

Figure 4.1 **Using Visualization to Remember U.S. Geography**

2. *Chunking information*: This strategy groups like items together to facilitate memory. The groups should include items in the same category or classification. An example of this strategy is to organize a grocery list with all of the produce in one group and all of the dairy in another. Sub-chunking (listing all fruits and vegetables separately for example) may be needed if the lists are long. To practice chunking information to learn the states in the U.S., you could group the states by region, beginning with the area in which the student lives. For example, if the student lives in Florida, she could start by grouping the southeastern states, then the northeastern states, and so forth.

© 2007, Rhona M. Gordon, Thinking Organized. All Rights Reserved. Duplication Prohibited.

Figure 4.2 **Using Acronyms to Remember U.S. Geography**

3. ***Mnemonic devices***: We all use this memorization strategy in different ways. Here are some tricks that are successful for the disorganized thinker.

   - ***Acronym***: Take the first letter of each item to be remembered and put it into a new word. A familiar acronym is "HOMES" which represents the first letter in the names of the Great Lakes: H - Huron; O - Ontario; M - Michigan; E - Erie; and S - Superior. You can manipulate the letters to create a name that one will more easily remember. For example, instead of remembering the three West Coast states of Washington, Oregon, and California as "W-O-C," start from the bottom of the map to create "C-O-W." (See figure 4.2 above.)

- *Acrostic*: Acrostics help the student remember several words by taking the first letter of each word to be memorized and creating a sentence. A familiar one defines the order of operations for algebraic equations. "Please excuse my dear Aunt Sally" is the acrostic for these words: *parentheses, exponents, multiplication, division, addition*, and *subtraction*. It is easier to remember a meaningful sentence than individual terms that might seem random to the student.

4. *Linking information*: When memorizing a list of information, have the student try to put the words into a story form. For example, to memorize the exports of Somalia — livestock, fish, charcoal, and bananas — a student could remember the following sentence: "In Somalia, livestock and fish are cooked over a charcoal grill, followed by a dessert of bananas."

5. *Rhyme and rhythm*: Silly rhymes can help students remember uninteresting facts. Who can forget this one? "In fourteen hundred and ninety-two, Columbus sailed the ocean blue."

6. *LOCI*: This method involves location, using a common physical path and imagining the items to be memorized along the way. For example, a student could imagine the familiar path from her bed to the refrigerator. If she is memorizing the exports of Somalia, she could imagine livestock in her bed, fish in her doorway, clumps of charcoal in the hall, and bananas on the kitchen counter. Alternatively, a student could diagram a path through her neighborhood and then practice the sequence by walking it. Finally, one could practice drawing a path on paper, adding the individual items along the way.

© 2007, Rhona M. Gordon, Thinking Organized. All Rights Reserved. Duplication Prohibited.

Figure 4.3 **Using the Combination Approach to Remember U.S. Geography**

7. *Combination approach*: Although the student should be encouraged to try each memory strategy, often a combination approach is optimal. Try to engage the student in creating a system that works best for her and encourage the use of more than one technique. For example, use the map of the United States. There are five states in the middle of the country that are basically in a line: Minnesota, Iowa, Missouri, Arkansas, and Louisiana. If a student is not from that area, it may be difficult to remember where the states are located. First, use visualization and show the student that the states are in a line running along the Mississippi River. (See figure 4.3 above.)

Next, look at the first letter in each name to find a pattern, such as C-V-C-V-C (consonant - vowel). Create a meaningful acrostic for the student, such as "Minnie is missing and late." Two of these words can be found in the state's names; "Minnie" is used for Minnesota and "missing" for Mississippi. The other three states are represented by the acrostic: I for Iowa, A for Arkansas, and L for Louisiana. One fifth grader created the following sentence to remember these states: "My iguana makes awesome lasagna." Because she was fascinated by iguanas and loved to eat lasagna, her crazy sentence stuck in her memory. Five states were learned with one sentence! Remember that the sentence must have meaning for the individual so that it will be recalled more easily.

Play Memory Games

Luckily, memory games are readily available, making this skill easy to practice through play. A deck of cards can be used to play Concentration, where cards are lined up face down and the players take turns finding matches. Start by choosing pairs of numbers, such as the five of clubs and the five of spades. Initially, choose about four or five pairs to play with and increase the number of pairs as your child becomes better at the game.

Another easy game involves arranging a tray of small objects, letting the child look for a few seconds, then seeing how many she remembers. Start with no more than seven objects, and as the child improves, increase that number to ten. A variation would be to take two or more objects away, and see if she can tell you which ones are missing.

Everyday activities also present opportunities for

memory practice. Remembering phone numbers, addresses, or grocery lists are good for strengthening memory.

Practice attaching meaning when playing memory games. For example, when you pull into a parking space marked with a floor letter and a row number, such as "A4," ask the child to create a way to remember the location. One approach would be to say "A" is the first letter of the alphabet and there are four people in my family.

A game you can play in the car is the Alphabet Game. The first person starts with the letter A and says "A is for ___" filling in the blank with any word beginning with the letter A, such as *apple*. The second person then does the letter B, but must first remember that "A is for *apple*." So, the second person might say, "A is for *apple* and B is for *book*." As the game continues, each player not only adds her own word but also must remember all the words that came before. A variation is to confine the game to a specific category, such as food, famous people, or cities.

Remember

Securing information into memory takes time and repetition. Therefore, one should begin studying for a test or exam early and chunk the information to be memorized into manageable parts. Then, using one or more memory strategies, the information must be learned and repeated over time. It is crucial that time is saved to "over learn" the material. Making students realize that they need to "over learn" is a challenging task for parents.

STRATEGY 4: **MEMORY STRATEGIES**
SUMMARY CHECKLIST

The checklist is a guide to help you progress through each step of teaching memory strategies to your child.

❑ 1. Three kinds of memory — short-term, long-term, and active working memory. Need long-term for tests and essays, so save time to "over learn" material.

❑ 2. Ways to memorize material:
- Visualization: Use a mental image.
- Chunking information into like groups.
- Acronyms, such as HOMES for Great Lakes (Huron, Ontario, Michigan, Erie, Superior).
- Acrostics, such as, "Please excuse my dear Aunt Sally" for the algebraic order of operations (parentheses, exponents, multiplication, division, addition, and subtraction).
- Rhyme and rhythm: such as "In fourteen hundred and ninety-two, Columbus sailed the ocean blue."
- LOCI: mapping a mental pathway of things to be remembered.
- Combination: Often the best approach uses more than one technique.

❑ 3. Play some memory games with cards, objects, or the alphabet.

THINKING ORGANIZED HOMEWORK

Choose a memory challenge and use at least two of the strategies (visualization, chunking, acronyms, acrostics, rhyme and rhythm, loci, and combination) to memorize the information. Here are some ideas for the memory challenge:

- U.S. states. (One memory challenge could include seven to ten states, such as the Southeast.)
- Regional states and capitals.
- Five Great Lakes.
- List of foreign words.
- List of vocabulary words.
- Names of kids in your student's class (name all the girls or all the boys).
- Names of all the neighbors on your street.
- Your family genealogy: list the names of your family members, aunts, uncles, cousins, and grandparents.
- A section of the Periodic Table of Elements.
- Grocery list (make up your own).

Sample Memory Challenge

Here is a sample memory challenge for the divisions of the animal kingdom (in order): kingdom, phylum, class, order, family, genus, species.

- *Acrostic*: King Paul Cried Out For Guts and Slime.
- *Linking*: In the Kingdom, Sir Phylum's Class Made Order of Sir Genus's Species.
- *Rhyming*: Kingdom, Phylum Class Easies! Order Genus last the Species!
- *LOCI*: Walk around and touch the items to remember the bold words.
  - Bedroom is my **Kingdom**.
  - Pillow is a **Phylum** (both start with P).
  - **Class** is where I do my homework (desk).
  - **Order** is the filing system in my desk drawer.
  - **Genus** is the paper in the files (that make me a genius).
  - **Species** is the specific writing on the papers.

- ***Combination***: Figure 4.4 on the following page is a mind map for memorizing the organization of living things using an acrostic and visualization.
- ***Visualization***: Figure 4.5 is a mind map for memorizing the organization of living things with visualization.

Memory is one of the key foundations for learning. Picture a student who listens in a lecture and understands a concept that is explained to her. Without memory, she will never be able to access that concept again or use it in any meaningful way. Without memory, there is no learning.

Just like the muscles of your body require constant attention and maintenance to remain strong, memory needs to be exercised regularly to stay in shape. By showing your child how you use your memory for groceries, errands, or a parking space, you are demonstrating that memory is a lifetime skill to be exercised every day.

© 2007, Rhona M. Gordon, Thinking Organized. All Rights Reserved. Duplication Prohibited.

King Paul
(Kingdom, Phylum)

Cried Out
(Class, Order)

For Guts and Slime
(Family, Genus,
Species)

Figure 4.4 **Mind Map for Memorizing the Organization of Living Things Using the Acrostic and Visualization "King Paul Cried Out for Guts and Slime"**

© 2007, Rhona M. Gordon, Thinking Organized. All Rights Reserved. Duplication Prohibited.

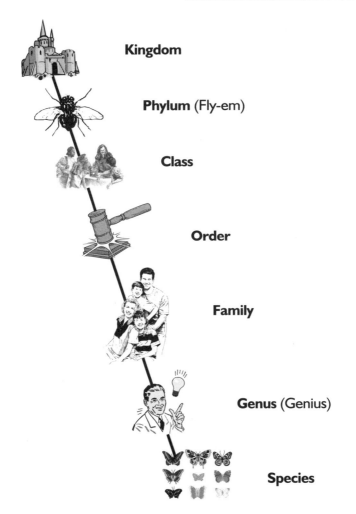

Kingdom

Phylum (Fly-em)

Class

Order

Family

Genus (Genius)

Species

Figure 4.5 **Mind Map for Memorizing the Organization of Living Things Using Visualization**

Toward Independence!

To help your student memorize information independently, the key is to teach her a variety of strategies and encourage her to use a combination of memory techniques. Practice is the only way for the student to learn which technique to use for different information. Sometimes drawing a map is more appropriate than a crazy mnemonic. By modeling your own memory strategies, for example with phone numbers or grocery lists, you demonstrate that memorizing information is a skill needed every day, at every stage of life.

Note-Taking to Improve Reading Comprehension

*S*cott spent a great deal of time reading his textbooks. His method of studying for a chapter test was to reread the chapter the night before the test. However, Scott found that sometimes he was just reading the words without really understanding the material. His mind would begin to wander and sometimes Scott would fall asleep. He did not remember enough of what he had read to perform well on tests, and his mother decided to intervene by using the Thinking Organized program.

She spent some time teaching Scott how to take notes

and create outlines using his reading assignments well ahead of the test day. They practiced using articles from his favorite sports magazine and Scott's textbooks. He realized that he understood the material better when forced to define main ideas and supporting details. Having a clear outline helped Scott brainstorm for possible essay questions and organize his ideas. By spending a little more time engaged with the material, Scott was able to weed out information that was unimportant as well as chunk information to store it effectively in memory. Scott used his notes to study for a test rather than rereading the whole chapter, which helped him remember more of what he read. Naturally, his test grades improved. Scott also reported spending less time studying, because he understood more of what he read the first time.

Taking notes helps the student better understand written material. As he creates notes, he is deciding what is important and what needs to be learned as well as condensing material into manageable sections. The student stays engaged with his reading material and focused on determining the main ideas and supporting facts. The act of note-taking can improve the student's reading comprehension and facilitate the memorization and integration of the material for a test or essay.

GOALS

The goal is to teach the student effective note-taking skills in order to further his understanding of written text. Delineating main ideas and supporting details helps a student become more engaged with difficult or uninteresting information by forcing him to think and take action the first time the information is read. Good note-taking skills are the foundation of understanding and remembering academic material.

PREPARATION

It will be helpful to have these supplies handy to practice note-taking techniques with your child.

1. Several sheets of lined paper, a blank document on the computer, or the note-taking section of the *Thinking Organized Workbook*.
2. Pencils or pens.
3. Social studies or science textbook, or any non-fiction text that is not too difficult for your child to read and understand.

REVIEW

The homework was to create a memory challenge along with a memorization plan. See how much your student remembers about the challenge and discuss which techniques were used. Review some of the basic memorization tools and encourage the child to use these strategies for many of his academic subjects.

Points or tokens can be awarded for the following:

- Assignment Notebook
  - Color coding is used.
  - Items are listed in the "Don't Forget" section.
  - Something is written in every subject.
  - The check/cross-check is used.
  - Extracurricular commitments are included.
- Binder Management
  - Papers are filed in the correct section.
  - Pockets are used for current work.
- Other Materials

- Daily check-in and check-out is used.
- Time Management
  - Guess/actual time sheet is used.
  - Monthly calendar has color-coded entries.
  - The student is wearing a watch.
- Learning Styles and Studying
  - Use one of the studying techniques used in Strategy 3. (Points awarded for each technique used.)
- Memorization Techniques
  - Memory challenge is completed.

GOAL 1: NOTE-TAKING SKILLS

In order to effectively understand a written passage, a reader must first be able to interpret the words on the page, understand the content, and have some general knowledge to reference the topic. The written passages used in this strategy should be within the range of the student's reading level so that the session is not devoted to sounding out the words.

Students with organizational difficulties rarely understand the considerable advantages of note-taking. Many feel that it is a waste of time because the information is already written in the book or in a handout. However, when a student does take notes, he saves time by understanding the material better and eliminating the need to go back to the textbook. When forced to take notes, the disorganized student may initially write too little or too much information. He tends to either see the "forest without the trees" or "the trees without the forest." This means that some students can determine the main idea but not find the supporting details while others can see details but have difficulty stating the main idea.

Therefore, we start by introducing the two-column outlining system in order to help the student divide information into main ideas and supporting details. Then we examine the Cornell Outlining System as described in Walter Pauk's *How to Study in College* to further divide information. There are many other note-taking systems available; however, during this course the student should not be allowed to deviate from the program. A student who presents with organizational challenges needs clear direction without options. Once the skills become habit, the student can substitute another outlining system, thereby individualizing the program.

The Two-Column Outlining System

In this system, a key word or phrase is put on the left side of the page. This is the main idea. The right side of the page is for the supporting information. Use one color for the main ideas and another color for the supporting information. See table 5.1 on the next page for an example.

1. ***Introduce visualization of information.*** This is a language strategy that teaches the concept of note-taking. To begin, choose a picture with very simple action, like one in a coloring book. A variety of images have been provided for you in the *Thinking Organized Workbook*. Ask the student to look at the picture and tell you in one sentence what the picture is about; this is the main idea. Next, ask for three supporting details. A specific number of details is important, because a disorganized student usually presents many details and no main idea or the main idea and a limited number of details.

    For example, the main idea in figure 5.1 on the next page is "A boy and a girl are reading and coloring

© 2007, Rhona M. Gordon, Thinking Organized. All Rights Reserved. Duplication Prohibited.

MAIN IDEA	DETAILS

Table 5.1 **Two-Column Outlining Sheet**

© 2007, Rhona M. Gordon, Thinking Organized. All Rights Reserved. Duplication Prohibited.

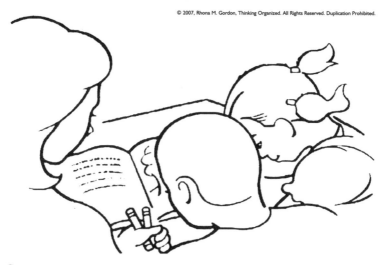

Figure 5.1 **"A boy and a girl are reading and coloring a book while the mother watches."**

a book while the mother watches." Three supporting details of the picture are 1) the boy is holding two crayons, 2) the girl is concentrating on the book, and 3) the mother is standing behind the children.

As the student becomes proficient at effectively describing the picture, practice with more detailed pictures from magazines or books. When note-taking on a more complex picture, more supporting details will be needed. If supplementation for the visualization process is needed, the Visualizing and Verbalizing Kit® by Gander Publishing (www.ganderpublishing.com) is recommended.

2. ***Practice note-taking by writing a two-column outline of a different picture***. Use figure 5.2 on the following page as a sample picture. Table 5.2 lists appropriate notes for this picture. However, feel free to use a picture of greater interest for your student.

Begin by writing the main idea of the picture on the left column. Ask the student to list three supporting details on the right column. Then review with the student to decide if the most pertinent information has been added to the outline.

3. ***Try outlining with the student's social studies chapter***. Social studies textbooks usually make note-taking easier by bolding chapter headlines and important information. Use a current assignment to construct a two-column outline comprising main ideas and supporting information. Again, use one color for the main ideas and another color for the supporting details. While teaching this skill, the parent will first need to help the student identify the main idea and supporting details. With more practice, the student will learn to take notes independently.

© 2007, Rhona M. Gordon, Thinking Organized. All Rights Reserved. Duplication Prohibited.

Figure 5.2 **Sample Picture**

© 2007, Rhona M. Gordon, Thinking Organized. All Rights Reserved. Duplication Prohibited.

MAIN IDEA	DETAILS
The boy is getting dressed to go outside to play in the snow.	Boy putting on his jacket Mom putting on his hat Scarf and mittens on chair Sled in front of boy Background: Snow falling Snow on tree and ground

Table 5.2 **Sample Two-Column Outlining Sheet**

The Cornell Outlining System

This form of outlining further breaks information into parts. The paper is divided into two parts; a third of the paper is folded on the left, leaving two-thirds of the paper for the right side of the page.

1. A main idea is listed on the left side of the paper with a key word or phrase. On the right-hand side of the paper, give an idea that supports the main idea on the left. Most supporting ideas have details that further explain the concept. List those details underneath the supporting ideas. Use different colors for the key word, main idea, supporting ideas, and details.

2. Some students can draw a shape or picture that represents a main idea or concept. This can be a helpful way to secure information into memory. One word of caution: a student may get caught up in the drawing and forget the purpose of the exercise. Use drawings sparingly until you know that the student understands how to take notes or you are sure that he uses drawing effectively.

3. Leave a two-inch margin at the bottom of the paper to write a one- to two-sentence summary of the information that was outlined above. This provides a quick reinforcer for the student and an easy way to review notes when preparing for a test.

Figure 5.3 on the following page is a sample of the Cornell Outlining System as described above.

© 2007, Rhona M. Gordon, Thinking Organized. All Rights Reserved. Duplication Prohibited.

There is a new kind of corn developed by cross breeding that could be effective in helping farmers grow better corn. In the past, farmers have had a difficult time raising corn, and they appreciate scientists' efforts to help them grow sturdier plants with better yields. The new plants grow quickly, thereby increasing productivity time. Because they are larger and fast growing, they are more resistant to bugs and other diseases. Each plant produces 30% more corn. Therefore, farmers get more corn per plant, more growing time, and less problems.

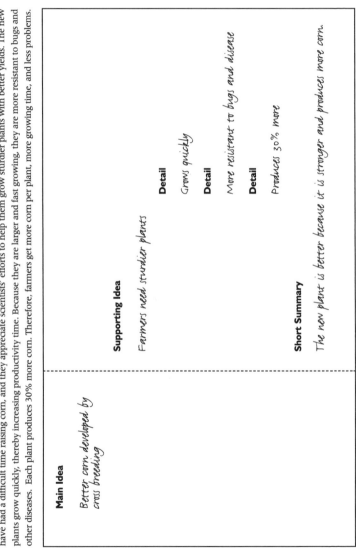

Main Idea

Better corn developed by cross breeding

Supporting Idea

Farmers need sturdier plants

Detail

Grows quickly

Detail

More resistant to bugs and disease

Detail

Produces 30% more

Short Summary

The new plant is better because it is stronger and produces more corn.

Figure 5.3 **Sample Cornell Outlining System**

The student who uses a note-taking system to read difficult written material has a considerable advantage in understanding and learning the information. Even the most complex text can be broken down into more manageable segments, thereby making the reading less daunting. Remind the student that practice is absolutely necessary to get good at this skill. Furthermore, when the skill is learned well, the student will save a great deal of studying time and increase his ability to understand and remember even the most challenging reading material.

STRATEGY 5: NOTE-TAKING FOR READING COMPREHENSION SUMMARY CHECKLIST

The checklist is a guide to help you progress through each step of teaching note-taking for reading comprehension to your child.

Practice getting the main idea and supporting details from a written passage by taking notes.
- ❑ 1. Two-column note-taking
  - Main idea on left.
  - Supporting details on right.
- ❑ 2. Cornell Outlining System
  - Main idea or key words on left.
  - Supporting ideas on right.
  - Supporting details on right. (Drawings are good too!)
  - One or two sentence summary at bottom for quick review later.

THINKING ORGANIZED HOMEWORK

Have the student practice the two-column note-taking system or the Cornell Outlining System on an assignment from school, or a social studies or science textbook chapter. See how much the student can do on his own, but do not hesitate to help. Remember that it takes a great deal of practice and repetition before a student can successfully take notes on his own.

My students who practiced note-taking in middle school and high school have reported that this is an essential strategy in college. Their peers who don't know how to take notes are at an obvious disadvantage with both lectures and reading material. As textbooks become more dense, the students who know how to take notes can separate the important facts and efficiently categorize material. In college, not only is the material more difficult but more reading is required. Poor note-takers experience a great deal of stress and are frequently found copying notes from someone else. Good note-takers are not daunted by dense, complex textbooks because they have a method for reading and understanding challenging material.

Toward Independence!

*T*o encourage independent note-taking, the student will need to decide which system works best for him, whether it is the Cornell method of outlining or simply jotting notes on the side of a text. Parents can model the skill with work documents or even an article in the newspaper. Reward your student when he is taking an appropriate amount of notes for the text he is reading, and soon he will have routinized this important skill for comprehending difficult material.

Strategy 6

Written Language Skills

*R*achel's teachers described her to me as an insightful, intelligent teenager. She participated in class discussions and often provided a unique outlook or opinion, which drew her classmates into lively debate. However, Rachel seemed to fall apart when faced with a writing assignment. Her history teacher reported that when they discussed World War II, Rachel was knowledgeable and passionate about her ideas. One particularly rowdy debate was followed by an essay quiz, asking the students to defend their opinion on ways the war could have been prevented. Although Rachel clearly had a strong opinion on the subject, she had considerable difficulty expressing her thoughts in writing. The teacher reported that during the quiz, Rachel seemed nervous, biting her lip and playing with her hair. In the end, Rachel turned in a short, vague answer that received a poor grade.

A student who is disorganized is often amazed that ideas form so easily in her head but become very difficult to put on paper. Writing is a challenge at any developmental level and as a student progresses through the elementary grades into middle school and high school, the requirements become more stringent. Having a specific pattern to follow gives the student a way to begin writing and helps her to produce a more organized essay. Learning to write a well-organized, expository essay is a skill that will benefit the student not only in school, but for the rest of her life.

GOALS

Effective written communication can be a difficult task for the disorganized student. In order to improve a student's writing, the following goals will be introduced:

1. *Pre-writing strategies* so that the student gets started planning her essay in an organized format.
2. *A specific writing structure* provides an easy-to-follow framework for the student's ideas.
3. *Preparing for an essay exam* will help the student produce organized essays that incorporate critical thinking and analysis.
4. *Writing a research paper* requires a student to integrate planning, researching, note-taking, organizing, writing, and editing skills.

PREPARATION

It will be helpful to have these supplies handy to help your child practice effective written language:
1. Several sheets of lined paper or a blank document on the computer.
2. Pencils or pens.
3. Index cards and a large envelope, if writing a research paper.

REVIEW

Even at this point in the program, there are some students who are still not completing the assignment notebook correctly or managing their time appropriately. These students often feel that the methods are burdensome and do not realize that by using these techniques, they will actually save time by becoming more efficient. If your student is struggling in this way, take time to review and stress the importance of using the Thinking Organized strategies on a daily basis.

Check the practice note-taking assignment from the last strategy, making sure there are clear main ideas and supporting information.

Points or tokens can be awarded for the following:
- Assignment Notebook
  - Color coding is used.
  - Items are listed in the "Don't Forget" section.
  - Something is written in every subject.
  - The check/cross-check is used.
  - Extracurricular commitments are included.
- Binder Management

- Papers are filed in the correct section.
- Pockets are used for current work.
- Other Materials
  - Daily check-in and check-out is used.
- Time Management
  - Guess/actual time sheet is used.
  - Monthly calendar has color-coded entries.
  - The student is wearing a watch.
- Learning Styles and Studying
  - Use one of the studying techniques used in Strategy 3. (Points awarded for each technique used.)
- Memorization Techniques
  - Student uses one of the memory strategies practiced in Strategy 4. (Points awarded for each strategy used.)

GOAL 1: PRE-WRITING STRATEGIES

When assigned to write on any topic of the student's choice, a disorganized student has difficulty knowing where to begin. Broad writing assignments without defined criteria can cause great confusion and frustration.

Creative writing asks the student to use her imagination to write a story with a beginning, middle, and end. Usually these stories have a conflict followed by a resolution and an ending that ties the loose ends of the story together. Disorganized thinkers may have difficulty structuring creative writing so that the reader can follow the story. Creative writing may be required throughout one's education; however, the student does less creative writing as she moves to the higher grades.

To write an organized, creative essay, a student should try to visualize the subject, as we've previously discussed.

The student who has difficulty beginning free-choice writing assignments may need to practice even more visualization techniques. If she has a mental picture of an item to describe, a story to write, or a point to prove, the actual writing process will flow much more easily. Once the writer learns how to picture an object in her mind and describe it verbally, she becomes much more comfortable with the writing process.

The student should also be encouraged to write about familiar situations or events whenever possible. Incorporating knowledge that is comfortable and well known to the student makes it easier to write because she actually begins the visualization process subconsciously. Remind the writer to use family members, hobbies, or daily routines in open-ended essays. Even creative writing is easier to accomplish if based in truth.

Expository writing is used to explain a point of view (explanatory), describe something (descriptive), provide an in-depth analysis (thematic), or argue a particular position (argumentative or persuasive). The writer must prove her point by using clear evidence from her broad-based knowledge, a textbook, literature, or research. It is essential that material in an expository essay be presented in an organized manner, because a reader does not have the opportunity to ask questions to gain clarification.

A student with organizational difficulties is likely to start writing without taking time to make a plan. Introduce one or more of the following strategies to get her started:

1. If the student has a topic, help her brainstorm ideas and write down three or four points she already knows. For example, if the topic is "The Benefit of Video Games," the student could describe them as "educational," "fun to play," and "something to talk

about with friends." By beginning with the easiest and most familiar part of the writing process, the student is better able to begin writing without frustration.

2. Another way to begin writing is to ask the student to talk about her ideas and have a listener write them down. It is important for the listener to ask questions in order to clarify the writer's point of view.

3. Model for the student how to ask questions to get preliminary ideas about a subject. For example, a student may ask, "Why do I like to play video games?" or "What do video games teach me?"

   An older student can use a more sophisticated version of the same technique. For example, a high school student may ask, "What educational skills do video games teach?" or "Do video games isolate children?" In the high school essay sample in Resource B, "Conformity Versus Rebellion in *One Flew Over the Cuckoo's Nest*," a student might begin by asking, "What is the author saying about rebellion and conformity?"

4. If a student has difficulty coming up with questions, introduce a CLOZE activity, as seen in figure 6.1 on the next page. The CLOZE procedure helps the student outline parts of an essay by developing key sentences with the endings left blank. In completing a CLOZE sheet, the student has effectively visualized and outlined the entire essay. Initially the parent will need to write the CLOZE activity for the child to use. However, by showing the student how to identify key concepts, the parent models the process of developing specific points for an essay.

© 2007, Rhona M. Gordon, Thinking Organized. All Rights Reserved. Duplication Prohibited.

VIDEO GAMES ARE WORTHWHILE

Three things I like about video games are _____,

_____ and _____. Two things that

video games teach are _____ and

_____. My mother likes video games because

_____ and _____. I also think video

games are a good thing because _____ and

_____.

Figure 6.1 **Practice CLOZE Activity "Video Games Are Worthwhile"**

5. Another technique for a student struggling to visualize a written project is to create a mind map (also called a web; see figure 6.2). In the middle of the mind map is the central concept of the essay, the basis of the introduction. Stemming from the central concept are the supporting arguments or facts, each of which may become the introductory sentence of a paragraph. The remainder of the web provides evidence and examples to explain each argument.

GOAL 2: WRITING STRUCTURE

Each student needs a structure for writing and it is best to provide the disorganized writer with only one system that she must use until mastered. When the student becomes comfortable with the writing system assigned, she naturally starts branching out and expanding the structure. Parents may feel that strict adherence to a writing structure could possibly stunt the child's creativity. Experience, however, has proven that lowering the student's frustration level by providing more structure better allows for the communication of ideas. Creativity develops after a writer learns to express thoughts clearly and fluidly.

Once the student has practiced a technique to begin an organized writing assignment, it is necessary to choose and review an appropriate writing structure. Even a young student can begin to utilize a format for writing that will make the writing process easier.

The Umbrella Method

Show the student an opened umbrella. The top part of the umbrella is the overall cover, just as the introduction of an essay

© 2007, Rhona M. Gordon, Thinking Organized. All Rights Reserved. Duplication Prohibited.

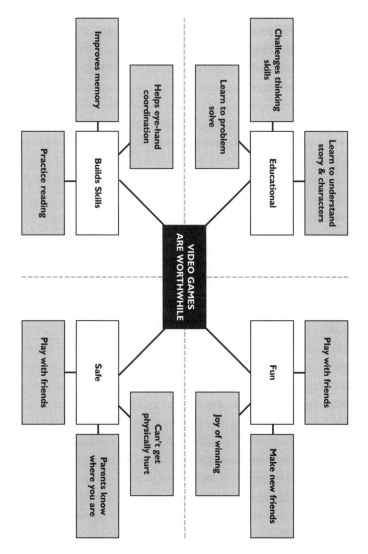

Figure 6.2 **Sample Mind Map "Video Games are Worthwhile"**

© 2007, Rhona M. Gordon, Thinking Organized. All Rights Reserved. Duplication Prohibited.

Figure 6.3 **The Umbrella Writing Structure**

presents the overview of the paper. Each individual panel of the umbrella is a main idea but needs the supports underneath. These are the evidence and explanations that connect each fact to the main idea. All the decorations on the umbrella are extras. In the same way that a student would add fringes to decorate an umbrella, she will add descriptions and details to beautify an essay. There is no umbrella without a handle. The handle unifies all the pieces to keep the umbrella tight and secure, just as a conclusion reiterates and combines the supporting facts to create an organized essay. Figure 6.3 illustrates this method.

For younger students, a paragraph can be modeled using the umbrella technique. The top of the umbrella becomes the introductory sentence, the supports are examples and explanations, decorations are descriptive details, and the handle is the closing sentence. Once the student masters the concept of a well-organized paragraph, she can expand on the skill by including more sentences in each paragraph that contain enriched vocabulary and additional supporting details.

Writing an Introduction

Academic papers require an introduction. In explaining to the student an organized approach to writing an introduction, it is helpful to have her picture a funnel, as seen in figure 6.4. Like a funnel, the introduction should start with a broad overview of the theme to be discussed. Next, the student should narrow the theme to the more specific topic that she will present. Finally, she will write the thesis statement.

Sometimes the thesis can be two sentences, but the student should practice incorporating the information into one. In the "Video Games" example (see Resource B), the thesis is "Playing video games can build academic and social skills while the player is having fun."

In the more complex example of "Conformity Versus Rebellion in *One Flew Over the Cuckoo's Nest*" (see Resource B), the first paragraph discusses the positives and negatives of conformity and rebellion and what one gains from each. The writer provides a general overview of these concepts for the

© 2007, Rhona M. Gordon, Thinking Organized. All Rights Reserved. Duplication Prohibited.

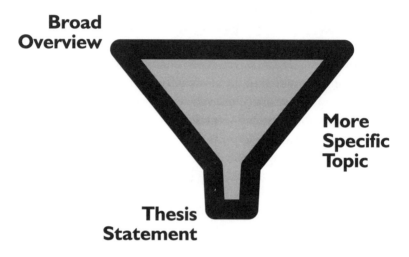

Broad Overview

More Specific Topic

Thesis Statement

Figure 6.4 **The Funnel Structure for Writing an Introduction**

reader. Then the student introduces her thesis: "In *One Flew Over the Cuckoo's Nest*, Ken Kesey uses characters and conflicts to present the dichotomy between rebellion to establish freedom and conformity to maintain security." Please note that when writing about a book, the student should always include the title and author in the introductory paragraph.

The S.E.E. Method (Statement, Evidence, Explanation)

The S.E.E. method is an effective strategy to help students follow a structured and reproducible approach to organized writing.

After the student has created a thesis, it is necessary to prove her opinion. This can only be done if the student integrates her ideas with specific information from the research material or novel. In order to make a solid argument, the S.E.E. approach is used for the body paragraphs.

- *S*: *Statement*. Make a statement about what is going to be explained.
- *E*: *Evidence*. Give evidence or examples from general knowledge, text material, or research.
- *E*: *Explanation*. Tell the reader why the evidence chosen supports the initial statement. This step is often omitted, but it is extremely important!

Before using the S.E.E. model, a paragraph must have a topic sentence. When writing the topic sentence, the student should ask herself, *what am I trying to prove in this paragraph?* The topic sentence must be an overview of what is going to be proven in the paragraph. In the "Video Game" example, the topic sentence "Modern video games incorporate many educational skills" is an effective overview because it introduces the aspect of education in a general way. This is followed by the more specific *statement* to be proven in the paragraph, "Some games use real life situations that can improve logic and decision-making skills." This sentence shows that the paragraph is going to give concrete *examples* and specific *evidence* that some games help improve logic and decision-making skills using real life situations. After the evidence is given, the writer *explains* how the evidence supports the statement. In other words, why was this example chosen? She should use specific details to tie the evidence to the initial statement.

Once each paragraph is completed, the writer should make sure that the development supports the original thesis. Even a brilliant idea that does not support the thesis should be saved for another paper. The writer should also ensure smooth transitions between paragraphs. The final sentence of each paragraph must logically lead into the next idea.

The paper must end with a conclusion. An effective conclusion will reiterate the thesis of the paper and suggest meaningful implications. If a student has difficulty restating her thoughts without repeating herself, she should look at each paragraph and state the main idea. Each paragraph's main idea can be put into a bullet point that will become the summary of the paper.

The second part of the conclusion requires the student to suggest meaningful implications, which can be explained to the student as the "So what?" Ask her to consider how her ideas apply outside the boundaries of the assignment, what insights she has gained, what questions the analysis answers, or what more can be concluded from the writing.

The last step of a written document should be the final check. A student may argue that her computer fixes capitalization and spelling errors, but point out the numerous ways that the computer may be wrong (for example: their/there/they're). Remind the student to carefully edit any errors in capitalization, spelling, and punctuation. Then have someone else — a teacher, parent, or student — review the paper. Adding a buddy-check system reinforces the need for this final review, which is an extremely helpful habit for any writer.

GOAL 3: PREPARING FOR AN ESSAY EXAM

Once the student can read a text and determine the main idea and supporting details, she is well prepared to remember factual information. Sometimes exams do focus on factual questions like "What were the causes and effects of

World War II?" However, as the student progresses through school, she is more frequently required to reach beyond the facts. Answering a question that requires the student to form an opinion, analyze information, or compare and contrast facts or events requires critical thinking skills.

There are basically four types of essay questions that the student should know how to answer. By learning the types of essay questions that may be asked, the student can be thinking about how to integrate information for an essay even when reading the text for the first time. This gets the student involved with the material on a critical level from the very beginning. The four types of essay questions are:

1. *Factual Questions*: These ask the student to describe, define, outline, or explain. For example: *Describe the events leading up to WWII.*

2. *Analyze and Interpret Questions*: These questions require the student to include facts but also ask the student to link information using some inferential thinking. For example: *Analyze the events leading up to WWII.*

3. *Opinion Questions*: These questions require the student to form a specific opinion about the facts and provide details to support her point of view. For example: *Why do think this happened*? or *What changes in events leading up to WWII do you think would have prevented an increase in hostility*?

4. *Compare and Contrast Questions:* These questions require a student to point out similarities and differences. For example: *Compare and contrast the events leading up to WWII from the perspective of the Axis and Allies.*

To effectively prepare for any essay question, the student can follow these studying tips:

- Determine the main idea and supporting details from notes.
- Practice preparing for sample essay questions. Sometimes, essay questions are found in the back of a textbook and sometimes they are supplied by the teacher. If samples are not provided, look at the main ideas and supporting details with your student, and brainstorm possible essay questions together.
- After orally brainstorming, help the student draw written connections. Many students benefit from showing relationships by drawing pictures and using different colors.
- Begin preparing sample outlines, using the S.E.E. structure of organized writing.

Critical thinking skills are usually taught in school. However, looking beyond the facts can be difficult for the student who tends to be literal in her translation of information. Every student would benefit from parental reinforcement of critical thinking strategies.

Problem solving is a great practice to encourage non-literal thinking in your child. One way to practice problem solving uses the student's favorite sports team. Ask her to imagine herself as manager of the team and ask her how she would help the team's rating to improve. She can begin with the facts she knows, such as the strengths of individual players and the team as a whole. The child will then be required to use these facts in a novel manner, brainstorming ways to change the existing structure to improve the team.

Discussing current events is another wonderful tool to help your student think beyond the facts. Dinner conversation could focus on a current event of the day and one family member might pose questions as to whether this current event is similar to any others; and if so, how; and if not, why not. Even while driving in the car, the parent could use an event from the child's day to encourage critical thinking. Asking the student to form an opinion and justify it, or relating a daily event to something else, will begin the process of non-literal thinking.

GOAL 4: WRITING A RESEARCH PAPER

A research paper requires more steps and more time than an expository essay. This can be daunting for a disorganized student, because she is required to collect information from various sources, integrate facts and data into an understandable paper, and not lose anything in the process.

Set a Schedule

Frequently, a student will procrastinate beginning a research paper because the due date seems so far away. However, the very first part of writing a successful research paper is determining the steps that will be necessary and developing a schedule to complete each part. Many teachers will provide written due dates for each phase of the paper (for example, the topic is due by May 1, research sources must be submitted by May 21, and so forth). If a schedule is not provided by the teacher, the parent must teach the student to develop a plan of her own.

To begin the schedule, plan backwards by first writing the due date on the calendar, even if it is more than a month away. Because it is a long-term project, use the color blue, as detailed in Strategy 1. Next, write down a date by which the rough draft will be completed, allowing about a week for proofreading and editing. Then choose when the research should be completed, remembering that some papers will require more sources (and therefore more time) than others. The last date to be assigned — but the first task to be completed — is choosing the topic. A working schedule could look like this:

Today's date:	April 15
Choose a topic:	April 20
Choose sources:	April 25
Go to library:	April 26, 28, and 30
Research completed:	May 10
Outline completed:	May 12
Rough draft completed:	May 20
Project due date:	June 1

Review Strategy 2 for more help in setting the schedule for a research paper.

Choose a Topic

Begin brainstorming ideas for a topic as soon as the project is assigned. Many students choose a subject, only to later discover that it is too broad or difficult to be practical. Therefore, be sure the student has time to narrow or refine the topic as necessary.

The best way to narrow a topic is by asking questions. If there are too many questions to be answered, the topic should be more specific. For example, a student may decide to write a research paper on video games and begin looking for information about different game systems, online games, who plays games, why they play games, how games were invented, how modern technology has changed games, and the future of gaming...and soon realize that there are too many questions for the scope of the paper. In order to narrow the topic, encourage the student to ask more specific questions. For example, "Why Are Video Games Good?" is too broad to reasonably research. A better question would be: "Are Video Games Educational?" A student could research areas such as improved memory, eye-hand coordination, and social skills to find information for her topic.

When your child has chosen a feasible topic, double-check a few more things. First, go back to the assignment and ensure that the topic focuses on the correct subject matter. Second, be sure that the topic is something of interest to the student. She is going to be spending a great deal of time with this subject matter! Last, check to be certain that the scope of the topic seems to be within the student's abilities. For example, the ambitious student who wants to discuss "How the Technological Programming of Video Games Affects Children's Long-term Psychological and Intellectual Development" could perhaps be led to an easier thesis of "Video Games Are Worthwhile because They Are Educational and Fun."

Research

Most research projects require more sources than just the Internet, although online is a great place to begin. Start with very general sources, such as an online encyclopedia, which will provide a good overview and summary of the topic. The student should schedule more time than she thinks she will actually need to complete the research. Sources on the topic may be difficult to find or extremely complex, requiring more than one reading or parental assistance. Material may need to be ordered from an organization or government office, which would require mailing time.

When gathering information online, it is important to

print the material. Even if researching at the library, send the information to a home computer to be printed. This can save time, because if it is not printed, the research may be difficult to find later or difficult to source for the bibliography.

Before beginning research, the student should divide her topic into logical sections. If she has asked questions in defining her topic, each question can become a section of the research. For example, "How Do Video Games Help Memory Skills?" could be one section and "What Are Examples of Ways That Video Games Help with Social Skills?" could be another.

Take Notes

Next the student must decide how she is going to organize her notes. The advantage of using index cards for note-taking is that they can be manipulated during the writing process, and the student can see where each idea or detail belongs. If note cards are used, insist that the student adhere to the following rules:

1. *One fact per card.* If there are two facts on one card, then when laying out the cards to plan writing, the card may need to be cut in half in order to have each piece in its proper place. Listing only one fact per card makes organizing the notes for writing much easier.

2. *List the source on the card.* It is a good habit to develop a bibliography while researching. As soon as a source is chosen, it should go on a list with a reference number or code (such as the author's last name). Then on the back of every index card, the code should be referenced. This makes writing the paper and completing the bibliography much less time consuming.

3. *Separate by topic.* Color coding is one method of visually separating research by topic. For example, all notes

relating to memory skills could be in red, everything relating to social skills in blue, and so forth. An alternative to color coding could be a reference number placed on the back of each card (for example, 1a) that relates to a list of categories (1a = memory skills).

4. ***Double-check after each research session***. It is best to have a parent check the note cards after each session, but if this is not possible, remind the student to do so herself. It is much easier to catch and fix a missing source when the information is fresh and accessible than to search for it later.

5. ***Keep it safe***! All research material must be maintained in one large envelope (or any type of folder that can be closed). Ensure that the student puts all note cards and printed material in the envelope at the end of each research session.

Keep in mind that some students prefer to take notes on lined paper. If so, buy a spiral notebook that will be dedicated to this one project. Have the student list her sources in the back page of the notebook and number each one. When taking notes, the number of the source used should be put next to each note. A separate page should be used for each topic. If preferred, a computer document can be used in a similar fashion.

Taking notes can be difficult for many students, as most would prefer to copy information and change the wording later. It is important to have the student put the notes into her own words as she first reads the text. This prevents accidental plagiarism and makes writing the paper much easier because the student has already processed the information and decided on its relevance.

Any quotations that the student may want to use to support a point should be listed below the statement and documented as a quote.

The student should take heart in the fact that when doing research, skimming a text is completely acceptable. Show her how to use the index, chapter headings, and picture captions to find relevant information. It is rarely necessary to read a whole book when doing research. Rather, most of the research is taken in smaller parts from several different books, articles, or online sources.

When relevant material is found, have the student read the source carefully, stopping after each paragraph to decide if the information applies to one of the topics. If it does, write a one-sentence summary of the information, add the source, and continue. For each note, the student should stop and ask these questions: Does this apply to my thesis? Does it make sense?

There is a great deal of potential for stumbling blocks during this part of the project, which is why extra time should be allotted. Frequently, research material that is applicable to a certain topic may be difficult to read and require the assistance of a parent or teacher. Sometimes the student has trouble finding information specific to her topic. Start early enough to be able to enlist the help of a teacher or librarian, or to revise the topic if necessary.

Preparing to Write

If note cards are used, the student should arrange the cards by topic to form a visual outline. The student who uses a notebook or computer document can create an outline using the main topics that have already been designated. Unless required by the teacher, a formal written outline may not be necessary, but it is imperative to have some sort of a written document (a web, bullet points, or an informal outline) to organize ideas.

Whether she is listing bullet points or creating an outline, the student should start by listing the main topics. Under each topic, list some general information and supporting details that explain the subject. Make sure the topics are organized in a logical sequence, and have a parent or teacher double-check.

Writing

When writing a research paper, there is no need to start at the beginning. It is often helpful to leave the introduction and conclusion for last, because these two paragraphs are not as formulaic as the body of the research. Start with writing body paragraphs, using the S.E.E. method. The statement may already be written from the note-taking or outline. Have the student ask herself, "What is the main idea of this paragraph?" She can then give evidence to prove the point. Evidence could be a direct quote, an example, or facts and details that have been researched. Finally, explain why the details support the main idea.

If footnotes or citations are used, it is helpful to put the code for each source into the body of the paper while writing. Later, the student can go back through and quickly substitute the source for the code that was used. It is imperative to notate sources of information during the writing process itself, as it can be extremely difficult and time consuming to identify the sources later.

Remind the student that when writing a research paper, she is the expert in the field. To help the reader understand her field, she must explain connections between information or give definitions for unfamiliar terms. For example, while researching video games a student might read MMORPG so many times that she forgets that others may not know that this stands for "Massive Multiplayer Online Role Playing Game." By defining the abbreviation, the student helps the reader understand video terminology.

After the body is completed, begin the introduction. Just as in the expository essay, the funnel structure should be used. Have the student begin the introduction with a general look at the topic and then present the specific aspect that will be addressed in the research. Finally, introduce the main idea or thesis of the paper, which is the main question to be answered. Figure 6.4 illustrates the funnel structure.

The conclusion is similar to that in the expository essay, which we discussed previously. If the research paper is attempting to prove a point rather than just provide information, the point should be clearly summarized in the conclusion. Next, the student should try to tie the research into something larger, such as a world lesson, or how the information could benefit society, or why others should read about the material that has been researched.

The final document, the bibliography, should be easy if sources were listed properly during the research process. Be sure that the format of the bibliography is correct by checking an MLA source.

Last, be sure the writing process is finished at least one weekend before the paper is due. Proofreading is an important part of a successful paper, and having a parent or teacher read and edit the document can help catch mistakes.

STRATEGY 6: **WRITTEN LANGUAGE SKILLS**
SUMMARY CHECKLIST

The checklist is a guide to help you progress through each step of teaching written language skills to your child.

❑ 1. Introduce techniques to help a writer get started
   Creative Writing
   - Use visualization to picture ideas for writing.
   - Writing about things that are familiar.

   Expository Writing
   - Brainstorming, writing out ideas.
   - Asking questions to get started.
   - CLOZE activities.
   - Mind map.

❑ 2. Writing an introduction
   - Picture a funnel that goes from broad to narrow.
   - Develop a thesis.

❑ 3. Introduce writing structure
   - Umbrella.
   - S.E.E. (Statement, Evidence, Explanation.)

❑ 4. Conclusion
   - Restate main ideas of paper.
   - Give a "So What?"

❑ 5. Final check
   - Grammar, punctuation, and spelling.
   - Transition sentences between paragraphs.
   - Use a buddy!

❑ 6. Preparing for an essay test
   - Determine main idea and supporting details.
   - Brainstorm possible topics.
   - Write sample organizers.

❑ 7. The research paper
- Set a schedule.
- Choose a topic.
- Research.
- Take notes.
- Outline.
- Write.
- Edit and revise.

Although writing can seem daunting to the disorganized thinker, the structures in this strategy can make the process much easier. Often students who initially have problems getting started and staying focused in the writing process excel when they learn to follow a specific format. Students who were previously intimidated by writing assignments find they are able to utilize their many ideas to make brilliant associations and conclusions. Writing well takes practice. Once established, the ability to write effectively will enhance academic success and become a valuable tool for the future.

Toward Independence!

*H*ow will you know when your student is independently using the structured writing techniques you have taught her? One way to judge is to review a paper she has written independently and highlight the S.E.E. (Statement, Evidence, Explanation) in each paragraph. If something is missing, it quickly becomes apparent and you will know the student needs continued monitoring. By rewarding your student for outlining information before beginning and for proper use of the S.E.E. system, you are helping her establish effective writing techniques that she can use throughout her academic career, and beyond.

Conclusion

You Can Do It!

*A*s the student has gained familiarity with all six strategies in the Thinking Organized program, it is now crucial to demonstrate the benefits of continuing to use the strategies in the future. Whenever possible, point out ways that time has actually been saved by writing down assignments and filing papers for each subject throughout the year. If your student still seems to be struggling, go back and review the strategies that are most challenging to him.

Students who accept and practice the Thinking Organized strategies do improve their grades, save time on assignments, and increase their self-confidence, thereby laying the foundation for success in their academic career and beyond. This has been proven over and over again in my own practice. I have learned that even children who do not use the program 100 percent of the time still benefit from increased awareness of the Thinking Organized strategies. Children adapt the structures to meet their needs; therefore even if they are not meeting every Thinking Organized objective, they still gain an awareness of the goal and develop a compensatory strategy for success.

For example, if a student is having serious trouble using the assignment notebook, he can develop another way to track assignments. Students who enjoy technology may be able to maintain assignments on a palm pilot or laptop. Another way to track assignments is to keep a monthly calendar on the front of the binder. The point is, not tracking assignments is not acceptable, but finding an alternative method can fulfill the goal and individualize the program.

Follow-up sessions are very important, and the frequency will depend on the student's mastery of the Thinking Organized strategies and his developmental level. If a child knows that he will be monitored on a regular basis, he is more likely to continue with the Thinking Organized program successfully. Here are some other ways to check and reinforce the Thinking Organized skills.

- Daily checks are helpful. Ask the student to go through his backpack while you are watching. Be sure that loose papers are put in the proper binder and the assignment notebook has been completed. Until the student can monitor his work independently, look at the assignment notebook and help him complete the guess/actual time sheet section.
- Weekly meetings are an effective way to check on

organizational systems, plan future work, and monitor any areas of concern.

- When asking the student about homework for the evening, get specific. For example, you could ask, "Do you have any tests this week?" or "What are you studying in Language Arts?" If long-term assignments are not already listed in the assignment notebook, have the student use his multi-colored pen to color code each task.

- Parents might use e-mail to remind their child of tasks that need to be completed.

- Online school reports can be a great tool for catching missing work. However, some teachers are inconsistent in keeping the website current. Therefore, students and parents should not depend on this source alone.

Although your child may call you a nag, persistence on the part of the parent can mean better grades and improved long-term executive functioning skills. Mothers and fathers are usually the best judge of how much parental involvement the child needs or can tolerate. As the student progresses, he becomes independent of parental help and more confident in his own ability to plan, monitor, and execute a project.

The Thinking Organized program is beneficial for anyone. Even the most organized person sometimes needs to restructure or revise his organizational systems. For the disorganized student — whether or not he presents with a formal diagnosis, such as ADD, ADHD, or language processing deficits — intervention with a program of compensatory strategies can mean the difference between failure and success.

When efforts are made to improve and expand executive functioning skills, individuals become more efficient at managing daily life. With enhancements in memory, word retrieval, and written language, communication skills are improved and frustration lessened, facilitating greater opportunities within the classroom or workplace. Thinking Organized establishes a firm foundation for learning success and instills strategies that can be used for a lifetime.

LET US KNOW!

The Thinking Organized program has been refined by years of working with students, and it is continually improving. If you have a suggestion or a question for Thinking Organized, please contact us through our website, www.thinkingorganized.com or by e-mail at info@thinkingorganized.com.

Modifications for Younger Children

The Thinking Organized program is designed primarily for students in grades five through twelve. However, most of the strategies presented can be used to establish effective systems for younger students as well.

Very young children are not usually responsible for their own organizational strategies. They depend on parents and teachers to establish systems and routines. In the early grades, many teachers use a two-pocket folder to send papers between home and school. The teacher sets up this system for managing papers and does not expect the child to track paperwork independently.

However, the earlier that organizational strategies are taught, the easier they are for students to use. Students who have been practicing organized thinking for years find that many of the skills come naturally when academic material becomes more difficult. Younger children are also easier to motivate and more willing to work with a parent. Here are some suggestions to incorporate the Thinking Organized program with younger students.

MATERIAL ORGANIZATION

Picture this: a three-year-old runs into the house and throws off her hat, gloves, boots, and snow suit. She is ready to go play in her room, but her parent stops her. The parent makes sure that the child puts the hat and gloves in a bin, hangs her snow suit on a hook, and stores the boots in the shoe rack.

Even in these little ways, a parent can foster effective material organization. Children should be encouraged to put their own toys away, preferably in dedicated bins, baskets, or shelves. If your own materials are a mess, don't worry! Instituting one or two systems (by establishing a place for snow things or toys for example) is enough to foster an awareness of the procedures necessary to manage materials.

TIME MANAGEMENT

Parents are the clock watchers for young children. Many parents give children a five-minute warning before they have to leave the house. This helps the child to transition from one activity to the next, and it fosters time awareness.

You can ask a young child to practice estimating time for fun and help plan family schedules. A calendar is another great way to teach time management to a younger child. She can start by marking her birthday, the birthdays of family members, and drawing pictures on holidays (such as a turkey for Thanksgiving). Holidays are discussed in school and this will further reinforce the skill.

If you are a parent that struggles with time management yourself, try setting one or two routines for your child. Knowing that laundry day is Tuesday or that bath time is at 7 p.m. are small reminders that can help make your child aware of time and how it is managed.

LEARNING STYLES AND STUDYING STRATEGIES

Younger children are usually taught by a multi-sensory approach. They are naturally predisposed to learn by using many different styles. A good example is learning the alphabet. Visually, there are many tools to help the child learn the alphabet: magnets, books, and computer games. Children are also taught the alphabet song, which is an example of auditory learning. A fun hands-on approach (kinesthetic learning) is to trace letters in sand or whipped cream.

MEMORY STRATEGIES

Young children love to play games and there are many commercially available memory games that appeal to preschoolers. First and second graders are often required to memorize spelling words. When helping a young child learn to spell unfamiliar words, make the activity fun and involve as many senses as possible. For example, one parent asked her child to write her spelling words on index cards and put them in various spots on the floor. The child would then jump to each word, say it, and spell it.

Several of the memory strategies discussed in Strategy 4 can be modified for younger children:

1. Repetition is important for any memory task.
2. Parents can help children use the memory skill of chunking by grouping spelling words that are similar in some way.
3. Visualization is another memory strategy that can be taught to very young children. Creating a visual image of the way an unfamiliar word is spelled can be facilitated by color coding the difficult part of the word, which is usually the vowel.

NOTE-TAKING FOR READING COMPREHENSION

It is extremely beneficial to help young children identify main ideas and supporting details. This can be done verbally or with the parent as note-taker. Start by using a paragraph from an easy-to-read non-fiction book, such as a biography. Show how the main idea is usually introduced in the first part of the paragraph, and pick out two or three facts that support the main idea.

The next level of reading comprehension that is helpful for even young children to practice is how to infer information from written text. Try practicing this by reading a fairy tale or fable to your child. After reading the story, ask your child, "What is the main lesson of this story?" Then practice finding specific events from the text that help the reader believe the main lesson. For example, in *Beauty and the Beast*, the lesson could be that beauty is only skin deep. Some supporting details are:

1. The beast is kind to Belle.
2. The handsome Gaston behaves inappropriately.
3. Belle chooses to be friends with the Beast even though he is unattractive.

In order to help young children improve reading comprehension, it is helpful to encourage discussions about what has been read. Ask a lot of questions about the material, the author's purpose, and how the material applies to the child's daily life. For example, for *Beauty and the Beast*, you could ask, "Is there someone you know who acts differently than the way he looks?" The more verbal interaction the child has with the text material, the greater her understanding. As she gets older, this skill will help her comprehend difficult reading assignments and be able to make logical conclusions with well-supported details from the text.

WRITTEN LANGUAGE SKILLS

The skill of visualization can build a child's descriptive abilities, a foundation that will improve her writing skills. Ask your child to open the refrigerator and choose an item to describe. Ask her to discuss the item's size, shape, color, food group, and taste. Encourage descriptive vocabulary. For example, if the child says, "A big red apple," keep asking questions. "How does it taste? What does it look like inside?" The end result could be a description such as, "A big, red, crunchy apple that has tiny, brown pits in the middle tastes delicious on a crisp, fall day." As the child's skill increases, show her how to compare and contrast items in the same category.

Children love to narrate stories when the parent types or writes for them. Creative writing is practiced in this way in early grades. Expository writing, which discusses a specific topic, is practiced less often with young children but is an important skill to foster. Writing about something the child knows is an easy way to begin. Creating a family newsletter is one way to give the child factual information to write about in which she is the expert. Articles in the newsletter could be about a pet, a vacation, or even an interview with a grandparent.

Resource B

S.E.E.
Samples

*T*he S.E.E. method is an excellent writing tool that helps students structure their thoughts as well as their essays and papers. S.E.E. stands for *S*tatement, *E*vidence, and *E*xplanation. The student makes a statement about what is going to be explained, provides evidence, and then explains why the evidence supports the initial statement. This method can be used in each paragraph of an essay. Once each paragraph is completed, the writer should make sure the development supports the original thesis. The final sentence of each paragraph must logically lead into the next idea. The examples in this resource section will help you teach this method to your student.

VIDEO GAMES ARE WORTHWHILE

Start with general look at topic

Present problem

Introduce main idea or thesis

Parents and teachers complain that video games are a waste of time. Often children must earn the right to play video games. However, video games can be considered good for children, and it is time to think about the positive aspects of this pastime. Playing video games can build academic and social skills while the player is having fun.

TOPIC

STATEMENT

EVIDENCE

EXPLAIN

Modern video games incorporate many educational skills. Some games use real-life situations that can improve logic and decision-making skills. There are several simulation games in which the player designs and runs a company, war, theme park, or household. To do this, the gamer must continually consider future consequences and think ahead of the actual play. * In order to be successful at these games, you need to make fast decisions based on logical consequences that you have learned not only from the game but also in real life.

TOPIC

STATEMENT

EVIDENCE

EXPLAIN

Another educational skill practiced in video games is memory. Most games require the player to hold information in memory while working toward the ultimate goal. Today's video games can have as many as 150 characters that need to be remembered and used by the player. Even if the game takes several sessions to complete, the player has to recall who is good and who is evil, as well as each character's individual strengths and weaknesses. Many times the player must keep in mind the large map in order to move his character to different places. When the gamer is required to remember information both during a game and from session to session, he is using repetition, mind maps, and visualization to memorize and recall the information necessary to beat the game.

TOPIC	Video games also build children's social skills.
STATEMENT	Children who play video games become less shy in social
EVIDENCE	situations. Most adults do not understand the language of
	video games, but knowing about a popular game gives
	even a shy kid confidence to talk to friends. Sometimes a
	gamer will become more accepted because he figured out
EXPLAIN	a secret to a popular game. When children discover they
	share an interest in video games, they have a common
	foundation to form a friendship.
Conclusion: Restate thesis	It is time to recognize that video games can help
	teach skills needed to do well in school, and can help
Then add meaning	children socially. Therefore, parents and teachers should
	not limit video game playing too severely, or worry when
	their children play a lot of video games. Maybe they will
	actually learn something!

(Note: In a student's actual essay, it would be necessary to mention specific games by name in order to provide proper evidence.)

REBELLION VS. CONFORMITY IN *ONE FLEW OVER THE CUCKOO'S NEST*

(Note: *The following is an excerpt from an actual eleventh grade essay. Included in this writing is the introductory paragraph along with two subsequent paragraphs that show the student's ability to use the S.E.E. structure in his writing. The essay has not been edited to perfection, but it is presented as an actual example of a student who previously struggled with the writing process and learned to create an organized essay by using the S. E. E. structure.)*

Start with general look at topic

Freedom is a concept that comes when one stands up for oneself and is not held down by the constraints of others.

Present problem

However, this freedom comes at a high price and no guarantees for success. One might be dissatisfied with the governing body or those who have direct influence over one's life. Rebellion can occur to gain freedom from unhappiness, or one can conform to those in control to

Introduce main idea or thesis

maintain the secure environment. In *One Flew Over the Cuckoo's Nest*, Ken Kesey uses characters and conflict to present the dichotomy between rebellion to establish freedom and conformity to maintain security.

TOPIC

One character in this novel can play the role of another person or a large group of people within society.

STATEMENT

EVIDENCE

The "Big Nurse" or Nurse Rachet in the story portrays the evil, suppressive government. She sets the rules and regulations that are similar to society's judicial structure. She shows the controlling side of the government and how the government keeps one in line in order to maintain control over the population. The nurse requires conformity from her patients. When one of the patients named Harding says, "You're safe as long as you keep control. As long as you don't lose your temper and give her actual reason to request the restriction of the Disturbed Ward, or the therapeutic benefits of Electro Shock, you are safe. But that entails first and foremost keeping

EXPLAIN

one's temper." (Kesey 71) This shows that the nurse, like the government, will punish you if you do not abide by the set standards. Just like the patients must conform to Nurse Ratchet's rules, citizens in a society must follow the

TRANSITION

law of the government. The characters in the story help to illustrate some of the conflicts in society.

TOPIC

STATEMENT

Kesey shows how conflicts in the ward mirror those of society. Freedom vs. Security is a large conflict in the novel. McMurphy wants freedom along with some of the other patients, but most of the patients prefer the security of the hospital ward.

EVIDENCE

The security is sometimes called the "fog". When the chief tells the reader that, "As bad as it is, you can slip back in it and feel safe. That's what McMurphy can't understand, us wanting to be safe. He keeps trying to drag us out of the fog, out in the open where we'd be easy to get at." (Kesey 123) The patients want the security that "the fog" provides in favor of the high painful cost of freedom. When the chief tells the reader about McMurphy's desire to watch the World Series the nurse says no. "This doesn't surprise him, coming from the nurse; what does surprise him is how the Acutes act when he asks them what they think of the idea. "Nobody says a thing. They're all sunk back out of sight in little pockets of fog. I can barely see them." (Kesey 114)

EXPLAIN

McMurphy is frustrated by the reaction of the patients and their unwillingness to stand up for themselves against Nurse Rachet. In McMurphy's mind the rules are arbitrary and only in place for the sake of controlling the patients. He feels that the Acutes should reject these illogical rules, yet he is disappointed when they stay in the fog. The conflicts lead to a clear struggle between rebellion and conformity.

© 2007, Rhona M. Gordon, Thinking Organized. All Rights Reserved. Duplication Prohibited.

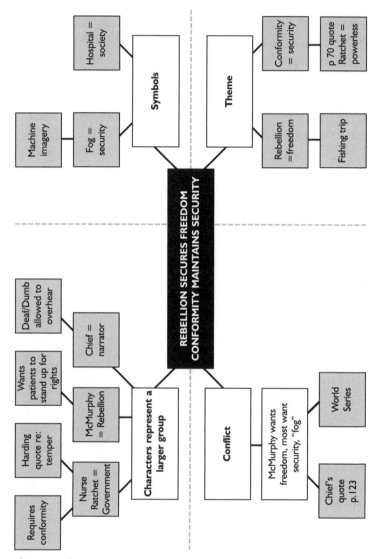

Figure B.1 **Mind Map: Rebellion vs Conformity in**
One Flew Over the Cuckoo's Nest

Writing Tips for Students

*W*riting can be intimidating for writers of any age. The simple tips in this resource section are tailored for three groups of students: elementary school students, middle school students, and high school students. Copy the appropriate tips and give them to your student to keep in a handy place for easy reference. Sometimes simply having a resource to refer to during the writing process can be helpful.

© 2007, Rhona M. Gordon, Thinking Organized. All Rights Reserved. Duplication Permitted for Personal Use Only.

WRITING FOR ELEMENTARY SCHOOL STUDENTS

1. To become a better writer, work on your ability to visualize and describe concrete objects, action pictures, and scenes in a book.

2. Another exercise is to pick two objects, describe them, and then discuss how each is similar and different. As you get better at this, you will be able to increase the number and complexity of what is the same or different.

3. When you are ready to practice writing a paragraph, try picturing the umbrella. The top of the umbrella becomes the introduction sentence, the supports are explanations and examples, decorations are descriptive details, and the handle is a closing sentence.

4. When you are ready to write an essay, try using these techniques to help you get started. Remember that there is a great deal of organization, both in your mind and on paper, that must happen before writing a great essay.

© 2007, Rhona M. Gordon, Thinking Organized. All Rights Reserved. Duplication Permitted for Personal Use Only.

WRITING FOR MIDDLE SCHOOL STUDENTS

1. To become a better writer, work on your ability to visualize and describe concrete objects, action pictures, and scenes in a book.

2. Another exercise is to pick two objects, describe them, and then discuss how each is similar and different. As you get better at this, you will be able to increase the number and complexity of what is the same or different.

3. Practice writing excellent paragraphs by using the umbrella. The top of the umbrella is used as the main idea, the part that holds the umbrella together. Next, the sections that support the top piece are the areas for supporting information. This section is followed by the more intricate part of the umbrella, like fringes, which are the details of what will be written. Finally, the concluding sentence is like the handle on the umbrella because it ties everything above it together.

4. Ready to write an essay? Get organized before writing! Using the umbrella technique, mind maps, or your favorite outline, always plan out your ideas before writing. Be sure each paragraph has an introductory sentence (a main idea) followed by supporting details.

5. Write the essay using the S.E.E. method.

6. Once the essay is written, check each paragraph to be sure it supports the central thesis and logically transitions into the next.

7. Next, read it, re-read it, and edit as necessary. Pay special attention to spelling and punctuation.

8. Use the buddy system to have a friend, teacher, and/or parent read the essay and make suggestions.

© 2007, Rhona M. Gordon, Thinking Organized. All Rights Reserved. Duplication Permitted for Personal Use Only.

WRITING FOR HIGH SCHOOL STUDENTS

1. What happens when you have difficulty writing your thesis statement? First, ask yourself what you are trying to prove. Write down all the ideas that occur to you and then begin crossing out the ones that are not applicable to your subject matter. Then look at all the ideas and try to condense them into two sentences, one if your teacher requires just one.

2. Get organized before writing. Using the umbrella technique, mind maps, or your favorite outline, always plan out your ideas before writing.

3. Write the body of the essay using the S.E.E. method (Statement, Evidence or Example, Explanation). Be sure each paragraph has an introductory sentence (a main idea) followed by supporting details.

4. Write the introduction using the funnel method. Begin with a broad overview of the theme to be discussed, then narrow the theme to a more specific topic, and, finally, write the thesis statement.

5. Write the conclusion by summarizing the main ideas of the essay and developing a "So What?"

6. Check each paragraph to be sure it supports the central thesis and logically transitions into the next.

7. After the essay is completed, read it, re-read it, and edit as necessary. Pay special attention to spelling and punctuation.

8. Use the buddy system to have a friend, teacher, or parent read the essay and make suggestions.

Helpful Contacts

NOTE:

The list of organizations on the following pages is provided by Thinking Organized for informational purposes only. The most current information at the time of publishing is included for each listing. Inclusion in this list does not necessarily constitute an endorsement of the listed organization by Thinking Organized. Readers should always consider more than one source for information. Thinking Organized claims no responsibility for the use of this list or any outcome as a result of using this list.

RESOURCES FOR HOMESCHOOLING

The Alternative Education Resource Organization (AERO)

The Alternative Education Resource Organization (AERO) is a nonprofit organization founded in 1989 to advance learner-centered approaches to education.

> 417 Roslyn Road
> Roslyn Heights, NY 11577
> Tel: 800-769-4171 & 516-621-2195
> Fax: 516-625-3257
> E-mail: info@educationrevolution.org
> http://www.edrev.org/

The National Coalition of Alternative Community Schools

The National Coalition of Alternative Community Schools is a nonprofit educational organization supporting the work of students, parents, teachers, and others in the field of alternative education.

> P.O. Box 6009
> Ann Arbor MI 48106-6009
> Tel: 888-771-9171
> Fax: 734-482-1867
> E-Mail: ncacs1@earthlink.net
> http://www.ncacs.org/

National Home Education Network (NHEN)

The National Home Education Network exists to encourage and facilitate the vital grassroots work of state and local homeschooling organizations and individuals by providing information, fostering networking, and promoting public relations on a national level.

> P.O. Box 1652

Hobe Sound, FL 33475-1652
Tel: 512-345-4895
Fax: 413-581-1463
info@nhen.org.
http://www.nhen.org/

National Home Education Research Institute (NHERI)

The National Home Education Research Institute's mission is to produce high-quality research and information on home-based education (homeschooling).

P.O. Box 13939
Salem OR 97309
Tel: 503-364-1490
Fax: 503-364-2827
E-Mail: mail@nheri.org
http://www.nheri.org/

EDUCATIONAL RESOURCES

Families In Schools (FIS)

The mission of Families In Schools (FIS) is to involve parents in the education of their children as skillful, knowledgeable, and effective partners, capable of ensuring that their children receive the quality of education to which they are entitled, and must have, to achieve life long success.

1545 Wilshire Blvd., Suite 811
Los Angeles, CA 90017
Tel: 213-484-2870
Fax: 213-484-3845
http://www.familiesinschools.org/

Gander Publishing

Educational products sold online

> 412 Higuera Street, Suite 200
> San Luis Obispo, CA 93401
> Phone 800-554-1819 or 805-541-5523
> Fax 805-782-0488
> E-mail: customerservice@ganderpublishing.com
> http://www.ganderpublishing.com

National Coalition for Parent Involvement in Education (NCPIE)

At NCPIE, the mission is to advocate the involvement of parents and families in their children's education, and to foster relationships between home, school, and community to enhance the education of all our nation's young people.

> 3929 Old Lee Highway, Suite 91-A
> Fairfax, VA 22030-2401
> Tel: 703-359-8973
> Fax: 703-359-0972
> E-mail: info@ncea
> http://www.ncpie.org/

National Education Association (NEA)

The National Education Association (NEA), the nation's largest professional employee organization, is committed to advancing the cause of public education.

> 1201 16th Street, NW
> Washington, DC 20036-3290
> Tel: 202-833-4000
> Fax: 202-822-7974
> E-mail: info@nea.org
> http://www.nea.org/index.html

National Parent Teacher Association (PTA)

As the largest volunteer child advocacy association in the nation, National Parent Teacher Association (PTA) reminds our country of its obligations to children and provides parents and families with a powerful voice to speak on behalf of every child while providing the best tools for parents to help their children be successful students.

> 541 N. Fairbanks Court
> Suite 1300
> Chicago, IL 60611-3396
> Tel: 800-307-4PTA (4782)
> Fax: 312-670-6783
> E-Mail: info@pta.org
> http://www.pta.org/

Parent Advocacy Coalition for Educational Rights (PACER)

The mission of PACER Center is to expand opportunities and enhance the quality of life of children and young adults with disabilities and their families, based on the concept of parents helping parents.

> 8161 Normandale Blvd.,
> Minneapolis, MN 55437
> Tel: 952-838-9000
> Fax: 952-838-0199
> E-mail: pacer@pacer.org
> http://www.pacer.org/

Parents Advocating Challenging Education (PACE)

Project Appleseed's nonprofit digital network helps parents and educators across the nation in the hunt for effective parental involvement

> 520 Melville St.

St. Louis, MO 63130-4506
Tel: 314-225-7757
Fax: 314-725-2319
E-Mail: headquarters@projectappleseed.org
http://www.projectappleseed.org/

Parents as Teachers

Parents as Teachers is the overarching program philosophy of providing parents with child development knowledge and parenting support.

2228 Ball Drive
St. Louis, MO 63146
Tel: 314-432-4330
Fax: 314-432-8963
E-Mail:info@parentsasteachers.org
http://www.parentsasteachers.org

Parents Helping Parents

Parents Helping Parents, a nonprofit 501(c)(3) public benefit agency, meets the needs of one of our community's most vulnerable populations — children with any special need and their families.

3041 Olcott Street
Santa Clara, CA 95054
Tel: 408-727-5775
Fax: 408-727-0182
E-Mail: info@php.com
http://www.php.com/

U.S. Department of Education (ED)

ED was created to ensure equal access to education and to promote educational excellence throughout the nation.

400 Maryland Avenue, SW
Washington, DC 20202
Tel: 800-USA-LEARN (800-872-5327)
Fax: 202-401-0689
http://www.ed.gov/index.jhtml

RESOURCES FOR LEARNING DISABILITIES

The American Academy of Pediatrics

American Academy of Pediatrics — an organization of 60,000 pediatricians committed to the attainment of optimal physical, mental, and social health and well-being for all infants, children, adolescents, and young adults.

141 Northwest Point Boulevard
Elk Grove Village, IL 60007-1098
tel: 847-434-4000
fax: 847-434-8000
E-mail: kidsdocs@aap.org
http://www.aap.org/

American Speech-Language-Hearing Association (ASHA)

ASHA is the professional, scientific, and credentialing association for more than 123,000 members and affiliates who are audiologists, speech-language pathologists, and speech, language, and hearing scientists.

10801 Rockville Pike
Rockville, Maryland 20852
Tel: 800-638-8255
Fax: 240-333-4705
E-mail: actioncenter@asha.org
http://www.asha.org/

ADDitude
Information and inspiration for adults and children with attention deficit disorder since 1999.

39 West 37th St., 15th Floor
New York, NY 10018
Tel: 888-762-8475
E-Mail: letters@additudemag.com
http://www.additudemag.com
Adhdnews.com

Support Group for ADHD Children and Adults
14271 Jeffrey #3
Irvine, CA 92620
Brandi@adhdnews.
http://www.adhdnews.com/

Attention Deficit Disorder Resources
A national nonprofit organization that helps people with ADHD or ADD achieve their full potential through education, support. and networking opportunities.

223 Tacoma Ave S #100
Tacoma, WA 98402
Tel: 253-759-5085
Fax: 253-572-3700
E-Mail: office@addresources.org
http://www.addresources.org/

Children and Adults with Attention-Deficit/Hyperactivity (CHADD)
CHADD represents individuals with AD/HD for education, advocacy, and support.

8181 Professional Place - Suite 150

Landover, MD 20785
Tel: 301-306-7070
Fax: 301-306-7090
E-mail: info@chadd.org
http://www.chadd.org

LD OnLine

LD OnLine is the world's leading website on learning disabilities and ADHD, serving more than 250,000 parents, teachers, and other professionals each month.

WETA Public Television
2775 S. Quincy St.
Arlington, VA 22206
Fax: 703-998-2060
http://www.ldonline.org

National Institute of Mental Health (NIMH)

National Institute of Mental Health (NIMH) Reducing the burden of mental illness and behavioral disorders through research on mind, brain, and behavior.

6001 Executive Boulevard, Room 8184, MSC 9663
Bethesda, MD 20892-9663
Tel: 866-615-6464
Fax: 301-443-4279
E-mail: nimhinfo@nih.gov
http://www.nimh.nih.gov

Glossary

Terminology

acronym: A word formed from the initial letters of a series of words. Example: SUV = Sport Utility Vehicle.

acrostic: A series of words in which the first letter from each word forms a name, motto, or message when read in sequence. Example: ROY G. BIV stands for the colors of the rainbow — Red, Orange, Yellow, Green, Blue, Indigo, Violet.

active working memory: Where information is temporarily held and manipulated while completing tasks such as listening, comprehending, or formulating a response to a question.

assignment notebook: A central source where all assignments and responsibilities are recorded.

Attention Deficit Disorder/Attention Deficit Hyperactivity Disorder: A neurological disorder characterized by lack of impulse control, forgetfulness, an inability to concentrate, and/or hyperactivity.

auditory learning style: The preference to learn by hearing or speaking.

chunking: Dividing information into smaller, similar segments.

CLOZE activities: A method of beginning the writing process by developing key sentences with a word or phrase left blank.

conclusion: The end of an essay or research paper in which the student reiterates the thesis of the paper and suggests meaningful implications.

Cornell Note-Taking System: A system of taking notes in which the main idea is written on the left side of a page, supporting details or pictures listed on the right, and a one-sentence summary at the bottom. Detailed in Walter Pauk's *How to Study in College*.

executive functions: The mental organizational processes where one can plan and sequence ideas or activities and then implement, monitor, and revise those activities as needed.

executive functioning weaknesses: When an individual experiences difficulties initiating, planning, organizing, and completing work. Frequently involves problems with attention, awareness of time, working memory, and cognitive flexibility.

kinesthetic learning style: A preference to learn by moving, doing, and touching.

language processing: The ability to process and understand language in verbal or written form.

LOCI: Mapping a mental pathway of familiar places in order to facilitate memory.

long-term memory: Where information is securely stored in memory and can be retrieved as needed.

material organization: The ability to properly catalog and maintain one's physical possessions.

memory strategies: Skills to help improve one's ability to remember.

mind map: A way to interact with material using pictures rather than words.

note-taking: The process of gathering the main or important ideas from a selection in a text and writing them in a brief format to study later.

S.E.E.: A method of organized writing in which the student makes a *Statement* about what is going to be explained; gives

Evidence or **Examples** from general knowledge, text material, or research; and provides an **Explanation** as to how the evidence supports the statement.

short-term memory: Where information is stored temporarily by using memory strategies such as mnemonic devices or repetition. The information is not retained unless put into long-term memory.

time management: An ability to be aware of the passage of time and to structure time effectively in order to accomplish daily tasks.

two-column note-taking system: A system of taking notes in which the student writes a main idea on the left column and supporting details on the right.

umbrella: A method of explaining organized writing. The top of the umbrella is the introduction sentence, the supports are explanations and examples, decorations are descriptive details, and the handle is a closing sentence.

visual learning style: The preference for learning by seeing or reading. The most common learning style.

visualization: The process of mentally picturing an image, item, or words.

Bibliography

Sources

Bell, Nanci. *Visualizing and Verbalizing for Language Comprehension and Thinking*. San Luis Obispo: Gander Educational Publishing, 1986.

Brown, Ph.D., Thomas E. *Attention-Deficit Disorders and Comorbidities in Children, Adolescents, and Adults*. Washington, DC: American Psychiatric Press Inc., 2000.

Dawson, Peg and Richard Guare. *Executive Skills in Children and Adolescents: A Practical Guide to Assessment and Intervention*. New York: The Guilford Press, 2004.

Frender, Gloria. *Learning to Learn*. Nashville: Incentive Publication, Inc., 1990.

Goldberg, Mel Elkhonon. *The Executive Brain Frontal Lobes and the Civilized Mind*. New York: Oxford University Press, 2001.

Keeley, Susanne Phillips. *The Source for Executive Function Disorders*. East Moline, IL: LinguiSystems, Inc., 2003.

Levine, Mel. *Educational Care*. Cambridge: Educators Publishing Services, Inc.,1994.

Levine, Mel. *The Myth of Laziness*. New York: Simon and Schuster, 2003.

Luria, Aleksandr Romanovich. *Working Brain: An Introduction to Neuropsychology*. Harmondsworth, UK: Penguin Books Ltd., 1973.

Lyon, G. Reid and Norman A. Krasnegor. *Attention, Memory and Executive Function*. Baltimore: Paul H. Brookes Publishing Co., 1996.

Pauk, Walter. *How to Study in College. (2nd ed)*. Boston: Houghton Mifflin Co., 1974.

Richard, Gail J. and Jill K. Fahy. *The Source for Development of Executive Functions*. East Moline, IL: LinguiSystems, Inc., 2005.

Richard, Gail J. and Joy L. Russell. *The Source for ADD/ADHD*. East Moline, IL: LinguiSystems, Inc., 2001.

Richards, Regina G. *The Source for Learning & Memory Strategies*. East Moline, IL: LinguiSystems, Inc., 2003.

Index

Topical Reference

Page numbers followed by *f* or *t* refer to figures and tables respectively.

About the Author

Rhona M. Gordon, M.S., CCC/SLP, is an American Speech and Hearing Association (ASHA) certified speech and language pathologist and an organizational specialist with over thirty years of experience. In addition to working directly with parents, students, and therapists, she has served as a consultant to public and private schools in the Washington and New York metropolitan areas. Rhona provides training, both individualized and in group seminars, to parents and school administrators on effective organizational strategies that can be used in the home or classroom. She also trains executives and associations on office organization to achieve a smoother work flow. Rhona is a frequent contributor to parenting magazines and newsletters and a presenter at industry conferences. Her affiliations include:

- American Speech and Hearing Association (ASHA)
- Maryland State Speech and Hearing Association
- Washington Independent Services for Educational Resources (WISER)

Rhona is a dynamic speaker with a great sense of humor and an enthusiastic personality that reassures parents and motivates students.

Make Thinking Organized even easier!...

The Thinking Organized
WORKBOOK
for Parents and Children

Now you can have instant access to every hands-on assignment in the Thinking Organized program. This workbook follows the Thinking Organized program and provides reproducible sheets at your fingertips. Once you have your child's attention, you'll want to make the most of your time by having all the materials at the ready. Worksheets for each chapter can be photocopied or used right in the workbook, saving time and aggravation for both parents and students.

Get personalized help at
www.ThinkingOrganized.com

- Schedule a distance consultation.
- Book a seminar.
- Join our mailing list to receive monthly tips and advance notice of new material.
- Find out more about the Thinking Organized community.